MEMOIRS

OF A

MUCK SHIFTER

Hector Mackenzie.

Produced by
Blaisdon Publishing
3 Park Chase, Hornby, Bedale
North Yorkshire DL8 1PR

Binding: Remploy Ltd, Stockton-on-Tees

This Autobiography relates to actual events and
nothing is intended to vitiate, or misrepresent any
real persons, alive or dead.

A CIP catalogue record for this book is available from the
British Library.

ISBN 1 90283838 6

Proceeds from the sale of this book will go to help the work of
Blythswood Care, Evanton, Ross-shire, Scotland, Christian
organisation for the care of body and soul.

Cover design: Bruce Webb

Dedicated to the memory of Papa and Mama
and my sister Eva,

and with grateful thanks to family members
and others who helped and encouraged me.

Contents

List of Illustrations

Foreword

*B*efore proceeding with my story, there are one or two things I want to put on record.

At the ripe old age of 78, whenever I meet new people and they ask me about my life, many of them seem to think it has been unusual and interesting. I suppose that is a matter of perspective. As I've grown older, there have been many times when I have longed to know a lot more of the lives of those who went before me. What I have written is therefore with family in mind, which may account for what may seem superfluous to others. Perhaps those who come after me may have some curiosity about my life. I have endeavoured to recount as honestly as I can 'My Life'.

Like every life it has contained highs and lows. Thankfully, it is mostly the highs I remember, but some of the lows can still kick in.

What I have written will contain a lot of 'I'; it is inevitable from the nature of my subject. Nevertheless, I would like it to come across with some degree of humility.

Early in my adult life I received a bit of advice – to make as good a job as possible of everything I did, and despite the fact that there have been many situations when my inclination was otherwise, the policy has stood me in good stead. Have a good read. I hope you will be able to laugh with me at some of my recollections.

For the completion of my story, I give thanks for the patience of my wife Julia along the way. If I have hurt anyone in the telling I ask forgiveness now. I suspect that in most autobiographies there will be one or two sequences that the writer's pride or prudence will cause him to omit. I confess that in that respect I conform.

Chapter 1

The Start and Before

*F*or me the start took place on the 7th day of March 1926 in Puerto Natales in Chilean Patagonia, but most new acquaintances take me for a thoroughbred native Scottish West Highland man. When the run of conversation leads to the name Puerto Natales, generally their eyes register blank bewilderment and I feel obliged to help them. Puerto Natales is located on the Chilean coast, hemmed in by a vast group of islands, (Archipelago de la Reina Adelaida) west and slightly north of the Strait of Magellan, and if you're still struggling, the latter separates the bottom (sharp) end of the South American mainland from the island of Tierra Del Fuego. For me, the question that usually follows is 'how come?'

As far as I can determine, my father Kenneth Mackenzie, better known to his contemporaries as Kenny Lachie, emigrated as a teenage shepherd boy from Ullapool in the Scottish Highlands to Argentinian Patagonia in the early 1900s. The name 'Patagonia' seems to have largely disappeared from the vocabulary of the current generation and from many maps of our day. I understand the word means Land of the Big Feet; if it were anything to go by, mine would confirm that. At one time, Patagonia was well known in the highlands and islands of Scotland. It consists of huge tracts of flat, mainly uninhabited land, the pampas, in the southern regions of Argentina and to a lesser degree in Chile.

During the nineteenth century many people emigrated from mainland Europe to the Falkland Islands and there, very successfully, took up sheep farming. A common reason for emigration is the hope of greener grass across the fence, or in this case, across the sea. And for them and for their sheep so the Falkland Islands grass turned out to be. In fact, so much so that the place became too small for them, and again across the sea, lay

Patagonia, vast, empty and eminently suitable for sheep rearing. Its respective governments apparently thought it of such little value that they paid scant attention to it. Although later contested, their separating borders were at that time scarcely defined.

One vital shortage in the sheep industry was that of skilled and reliable shepherds. Who more fitted than Scottish Highland shepherds, dependable men of integrity, often raised to Biblical standards, they and their dogs thoroughly competent, used to loneliness and with an added bonus, cheap to hire. A vital stipulation was that the shepherd must bring his dog. Thus, before WW1 did my father make the transition from the poverty of Ullapool to what he no doubt hoped was the 'greener grass' of Patagonia. In fact, it turned out to be a severely hard life, particularly in his early days. Living in Ullapool in my teens, I had been making noises of emigrating to Australia, and I remember my father in a letter expressing the hope that I would have an easier time than he did. In fact, I didn't emigrate anywhere.

The Highland shepherd, accustomed to handling at most about a hundred sheep, suddenly found himself in sole charge of a flock of several thousand, living totally alone in a tumble down shack, possibly 50-100 miles from the nearest human, just himself, his dog, his horse and no doubt a rifle – definitely not for the faint hearted. The only employer of my father I ever heard mentioned was a German, Mr. Wagner. In the absence of information, I now have to speculate what my German mother, Martha Juana Augusta Baumann, was doing in South America? It seems highly probable that she was on the domestic staff of the Wagner household. There was a marriage and on August 3rd 1922, my sister Eva Kenna was born, I myself following some 3½ years later. Puerto Natales, at one time a penal settlement, seems to have been the nearest place with some degree of services where an expectant mother from our part of Argentinian Patagonia might resort to for the birth of her child.

There is a touching incident from the region, of another Ullapool family – the Macleans. This took place in the early 1930s. While

Mrs. Maclean, alone, was driving her seriously ill husband through the wilds, hoping for help in Puerto Natales, he died in the car en route. She was left widowed in a strange land with eight of her family. They were my contemporaries; later she and her family moved to Ullapool.

It is quite hard to distinguish between infant memory and sights of old photos over the years. From family photograph albums of the time, it is apparent that our home was a rather nice looking large bungalow with corrugated iron roof. Faint memories arise of a roomy custom-built playpen, which I occupied. The style of house was confirmed some 70 years later in a well-researched television documentary, which showed a preserved house typical of the residence of an estancia (ranch) manager of my father's time. The life style had become reasonably comfortable but seriously isolated. Our nearest neighbours lived 50 miles away. The homestead was not far from a large lagoon and therefore was called Estancia Laguna Larga. Also the river Rio Turbio flowed through the land. Its name seems to have been with good reason. Family photograph albums show a substantial looking bridge, also a picture of the scene with the same bridge swept away and replaced by a makeshift arrangement of farm carts locked end to end to bring a flock of sheep over the Rio Turbio. Pictures showed large strong looking sheep; I guess they would need to be, since there are other shots of a flock virtually buried in snow. The climate was extreme, alternating between very hot summers and near sub-Antarctic winters. Life there centred heavily on sheep. So profuse were they and so remote were we that, in my childhood, I recall hearing that when my mother required ingredients entailing kidneys for the family meal, my father simply had the appropriate animals slaughtered, kidneys went to the kitchen, and the remainder disposed of, perhaps for dog food.

Life must have been tough for Mama, and in God's providence it never appears to have eased. I suspect she was a gentle person and probably a Christian.

Estancia Laguna Largo, Patagonia

Papa

Tante & Mama

Father breaking in a horse

Winter

Mama & Papa ~ 1921

Mama & Eva

Sledging with Tante

Mama, Tante, Eva and me

Recently I met and chatted with a lady whose family were our neighbours in Patagonia. She told me that her late mother described Mama as the most lovely lady she had ever known.

* * *

Certainly Eva and I were taught a child's prayer, which we recited in German, kneeling at our bedsides, now in Scotland, which almost brings us to the next 'how come?' I cannot leave Patagonia without reference to other family photos. My mother's sister Ida Baumann started to appear in family groups. The sisters were handsome and presentable looking women. Then there was Soto, heavily moustached and strong looking, I guess with plenty Spanish blood, probably a family retainer. He appeared, holding by the bridle the horse, which I, aged two, was unsuccessfully trying to straddle.

Early riding lesson from Papa ~ Jan 1929

Once more I speculate; had Mama become the victim of what we now call post-natal depression, had the remote and austere life become too much for her? There are none now alive who can tell me. Papa had to make mighty decisions. I still sorrow for him. In the UK spring of 1929, (Patagonian seasons were opposite to UK), the family, minus papa and in the temporary care of Aunt Ida (we referred to her simply as Tante), sailed east across the Atlantic on S.S. *Rhodopus*, most likely sailing from the port of Rio Gallegos near the bottom end of the Argentinian east coast. My third birthday occurred on the voyage. Old photos show games of deck quoits and a deck cargo of horses in individual box stalls. Beyond that, I remember little of the voyage apart from one day being taken by Tante with Eva to Mama's dark cabin where she lay in her bunk. I think the visit was short and the talk scanty. That was the last I remember seeing of Mama.

Then one sunny day we were tied up at a quay in the port of Antwerp, and standing on a handsome chair, I was able to see over the ship's rail.

I watched fascinated as Tante directed my gaze to a stream of various coloured motor vans scurrying by on the dockside street below. I had neither knowledge, nor, as far as memory serves, concern for what came next.

What did come next was disembarkation at the port of Hamburg. It never seemed to rain, or perhaps I remember only the sunny bits. There I was in Hamburg, happy as the proverbial sand boy, playing in a Hamburg

Arriving in Antwerp

19

children's sandpit with a little German boy Gunter, who I suspect was one of the welcoming party. All was well till the adults noticed that Gunter had 'scarpered'. There he was, gone, as one might say, happily not for too long. He was retrieved from some interesting shop fronts round the corner – my last acquaintance with Gunter. Memory suggests very strongly a sightseeing trip on a 'water bus' on the river Elbe. I don't know what the Germans called their boats, but they were the equivalent of the French '*bateau mouche*' on which I once had the pleasure of enjoying a trip on the River Seine at Paris one afternoon during a one-day visit.

Mama had a second sister, Lizzy Baumann, who was married to farmer uncle Albert Lembek. Their two children, Willie and Martha, were contemporary with Eva and me, and we seemed to have a happy few months on their 'Oldenbush' farm, I guess somewhere in north-east Germany. As a matter of interest, or perhaps no interest, I have been given to understand that my Baumann grandfather had been a member of the personal bodyguard of Kaiser Wilhelm the Second (of 1914-18 ill-repute). But, back to Oldenbush – for years afterwards, every time I savoured the unique smell of horses, my mind involuntarily returned to riding in beautiful sunshine through the peaceful German countryside, safely installed in uncle Albert's two-horse four-wheel buggy, the family transport.

As I grew in thought capability, it was Eva with her age advantage who in course of time brought me up to date on the main purpose of our visit to Germany, namely for Mama to be committed to a home in the town of Greifswald. There, poor Mama stayed till her death in 1938 – dying whether from natural causes, or the well-known Nazi programme of euthanasia for those considered of no further use to the state, I shall never know. Aged 12, although I had never consciously known her, when the news was broken to me I wept copiously, and in the custom of the time, was required to wear a black band on my jacket sleeve.

Riding in Uncle Albert's Buggy

For real trauma, we have to return to the Lembek family. Nazi-ism had swiftly come to power in Germany, then came World War Two. Now 13 years old and starting to pay attention to newspapers and adult talk, and on an odd occasion being derided for my part-German origin, I accepted the reported extraordinary evil of the Germans. It was Eva who, when our cousin Willie Lembek became a prisoner of war in England, visited him bearing small gifts. Somehow she remained in communication with, and after the war several times visited Tante in Hamburg. Later, we learned that Willie's sister Martha had married a Nazi; with the arrival of the Russians, uncle Albert disappeared into the maw of Russian Siberia, was never heard of again, and somewhere along the line, Aunt Lizzie had taken her own life.

It's time to introduce to you members of papa's family, first his father Lachlan Mackenzie an Ullapool carter. A carter was one who earned a livelihood plying his heavy horse pulling a small sturdy two-wheeled cart, the standard haulage unit of the day. I remember them from the 1930s as they distributed coal to the Ullapool homes, from the Clyde 'puffers' tied up at the pier.

Next, Lachlan's wife, my grandmother Jane (née) Macdonald from Strath Kanaird, a small crofting settlement eight miles north from Ullapool. She and Lachlan were married in Ullapool Free Church (now Ullapool Church of Scotland) on the 25th December 1884. They had a family of four, Margaret born in 1885 and who will turn up again as aunty Maggie.

We didn't have aunts. Aunts tended to be on the posh side; we had aunties. In 1929 on our arrival at Ullapool, aunty Maggie became guardian to Eva and myself. From official registers, all four of Lachlan and Jane's family were born at a house on Pultney Street, Ullapool. The houses on Pultney Street, in common with other parts of the village, did not have running water. In fact most houses drew their water supplies from three or four strategically placed outdoor heavy cast iron outlets with heavy screw valve controls. These remained until some time after World War Two. Later, the Lachie family moved to the last house on the right before the Ullapool museum on Argyle St. – the said house is now a Chemist's shop.

But, back to the family. Margaret Mackenzie, (Aunty Maggie) the eldest, better known locally as Maggie Lachie, apart from one visit to Canada, followed by one to Germany, lived and died a spinster in Ullapool. In those days, it was customary for individuals to be referred to by their Christian name usually followed by the father's name or often simply by his nickname, which in the small communities were profuse.

Hence Maggie's siblings were Kenny Lachie (my father), his twin brother Colin Lachie and lastly, Murdo Lachie (Uncle Murdo), the youngest. I can only guess that probably about the same time as my father's move to Patagonia, his twin Colin emigrated to Canada. He had something of a reputation as a runner and was often referred to as 'Speedy'. He had what must have been a short career in banking, I think in Winnipeg where in the 1920s, Maggie visited him and his family.

Colin had married and had two sons, Bruce and Gordon. Sadly on the day Eva and I arrived in Ullapool, his mother Jane received the news of his sudden and early death. Bruce and Gordon became wheat farmers on the great Canadian prairie land. Thereafter, correspondence between the family and Ullapool was infrequent.

In 1941 or '42, Bruce made contact with the Ullapool family. He was now flying in the RAF and wanted to visit during a period of leave. Uncle Murdo met him at Garve railway station. Later, Bruce said that he instantly recognised Murdo from his resemblance to his father. Eva, now resident in Glasgow, corresponded with Bruce for some years afterwards, but then all contact came to an end.

Popping back to Maggie for a moment – in her young days she had trained as a dressmaker in Glasgow and very skilful she was. Somehow she had never married. At the age of 45 she became saddled with us two little children to raise – and also her widowed mother Jane, a staunch Free Presbyterian Christian, and very much a matriarch. In my old age, I have at last come to realise what a now unpayable debt I owe them. Thankfully, prior to my arrival in Ullapool, Papa, then making money, had financed for them and us the purchase of two properties on Argyle St., backed by a third one accessing onto Pultney St. Murdo was set up in business with a large wooden garage on Pultney St. and a spanking new *Dodge* (Motors) seven-seat car for hire work. In those days, a car of any kind, never mind a new one was quite something in Ullapool. I understand it was known locally as the travelling sitting room.

It was in the *Dodge* in 1929 that Eva and I, accompanied by Tante and Aunty Maggie made the first part of our journey from Inverness railway station to Ullapool. Somewhere en route, we were met by Uncle Murdo with a smaller car, a 4/5-seater fabric bodied *Austin*. Nowadays, both the *Dodge* and the *Austin* would be prized vintage models. I can still just about feel and smell the beautiful leather upholstery, especially of the *Austin*.

An old man in the village told me he could remember Uncle Murdo as a very young man, working with a horse and cart hauling 'bottoming' (foundation stones) at Inchbeah for the upgrading of the Garve-Ullapool road. Whether before or after that, I cannot tell, Uncle Murdo served with the Seaforth Highlanders in the trenches in France, 1914 – 1918. Eva said he had been slightly gassed. And that brings to mind stories of German prisoners of war from some nearby camp washing their dishes in the Black Water River near Inchbeah. There had also been German POWs felling the woods at Braemore, about eleven miles out of Ullapool.

Lachlan & Jane Mackenzie; probably early 1920s.
Guanaco skin from Patagonia

Chapter 2

Brown Boots, Leith and Ullapool.

*I*t was still good weather when the move came from Oldenbush to Ullapool. In late summer or autumn, Aunty Maggie had come to Germany to collect her new charges. Probably to lessen the trauma for Eva and myself, Tante accompanied us. Again we sailed on a German ship, SS. Weimar, taking us from Hamburg to Leith, and from Edinburgh we went by steam train to Inverness.

I think one of the great sorrows of 'progress' is the passing into history of steam trains. I still thrill to the memory of my carriage's surges forward to each thrust of the engine's pistons as the train accelerated away from a station.

I have already mentioned our transportation from Inverness to Ullapool, where in quick order I was set reluctantly upon Grandma Jane's bony and black clad lap. She was a widow after all, and from widowhood to death, no matter how early in marriage the husband had died, the standard garb for a widow was black. It was probably a joy for her on this day of sudden bereavement of her son Colin, to have 'hands on' the small son of her other long-departed twin son, Kenny. I am still just about aware of grandma undoing my high-laced brown German boots. I have the impression that they were deemed unsuitable for my tender years. On reflection, it must have been an interesting scene and conversation, Eva and I speaking German with a few words of Spanish thrown in, Tante speaking German with, I suspect, bits of inadequate English, and the rest of the household and any callers, bilingual English/Gaelic but majoring on Gaelic

We appear to have been well clad with our boots and overcoats, all spruced up and Eva with a ribbon in her hair. We were also well equipped; Eva had a substantial and well-dressed doll and I with three bits of gear, namely, my large dark brown teddy bear – I think of German origin – Snooker, my white furry elephant on small wheels – he had a smart dark green velvet and gold trimmed cover on his back. Then, last but not least, Hissy, a floppy-eared rabbit on eccentrically mounted wheels, which, as he moved along, caused him to bob up and down just like the real thing. He had come with me from Patagonia.

Tante stayed with us in Ullapool for some time. I recall black and white photos from the time, of picnic groups in which she featured. I don't recall Tante's departure; perhaps we were shielded from it. But throughout our childhood, she never forgot our birthdays, Christmas or Easter, each of which brought from Germany a really worthwhile parcel containing interesting toys and delicious marzipan preparations. The foundations of life are laid early; I have never lost my desire for and appreciation of marzipan. By the grace of God, life went on and I suppose during the following period, the foundations of my still incomplete knowledge of the Gaelic language were laid. Many a laugh I still raise as I struggle to converse with Julia (my second wife) in her native language.

Adult conversation in the household at Rosebank was mainly in Gaelic and to get to know what was going on about us or impending, it was a natural for Eva and myself to quickly acquire a working knowledge. Eva, aged seven, must have been soon introduced to the local school, primary and secondary in one building, and with a high educational standard which could take suitable students direct to university. The Lachie household budget was augmented by accommodating two of the female teachers as boarders. Considering her initial language handicap, Eva must have had a rather good I.Q. Pretty soon she took top position in her class and remained so, or close to it, right up to university standard.

It must have been for my fourth birthday that I received the gift of a beautifully handmade and scaled down hand-barrow. It was an exact replica of the one Uncle Murdo used for domestic work, including the mucking out of the family cow's byre and in season, for forwarding the amassed products to the kitchen garden to fertilise the next crop of potatoes and veg., some of which would in due course find its way back to the original donor in its feed.

I remember vividly an occasion when as we took our meal at the large kitchen table, Grandma suddenly shooting up, grabbing her stick, and with a string of mainly respectable Gaelic imprecations, charging out the back door to deal with the ignorant cow, who had made her way uninvited into the garden and was contentedly enjoying a meal of choice spring cabbage. The family also had a small flock of domestic hens that theoretically were kept in order by their arrogant Rhode Island cockerel who strutted about among them; but often there had to be human intervention when the more determined of the flock found their way to the tender pickings of the kitchen garden.

In those pre-TV, pre-radio and largely pre-telephone days, there was a good deal of house visiting engaged in by the women of the village. Frequently, Aunty Maggie took me on these afternoon jaunts; I'm sure showing me off with satisfaction. I have not forgotten the discomfort if not pain of trotting at her side with my hand and arm held aloft by her hand, her elbow at ninety degrees. I suffered in silence, but I have never forgotten the lesson. As an adult taking small children including my own by the hand, I've always made sure that my hand was lowered to a suitable level for them.

The memory of one of our afternoon jaunts stays with me. All domestic cooking and heating was by direct coal or peat fire. We were welcomed into friend Etta's house; the open range fire had gone dull and Etta quickly sought to revive it by simply throwing on a generous splash of liquid, paraffin or petrol I know not, but the result was dramatic. As the fluid hit the hot fire, it ignited and a mighty whoosh of flame shot out at my face level and in my direction. I cried out in terror, but Etta seemed undisturbed.

In time, I graduated to walking the near streets on my own. Well, not entirely; I was usually pulling my barrow by its handles and with Snooker and Hissy trundling tied on in line astern. The Ullapool street traffic of those days was slow and minimal in quantity. Paedophilia had never been heard of in Ullapool. Little children could roam the streets in safety, virtually in the charge of all five hundred of the population. Most people I met on my travels would stop for a chat; some adult pockets carried a little store of sweets for these occasions; old ladies would invite me in for a biscuit. Thus I made my acquaintance with old Charlie Fraser and his dear wife, who lived in Myrtle Cottage on Argyle Street.

I learned that if I went along to the Post Office when I saw Charlie's big grey mail bus there, around 3.30 in the afternoon, I would be set fair for a ride in it up to its garage behind the Royal Hotel. I eagerly took up this excellent perk. To add cream to the cake, after I had pattered and chattered my way beside Charlie back to Myrtle Cottage, Mrs Charlie seldom failed to come up with a sweet or biscuit and gentle talk.

Later in life, it became known to me that Charlie was the last surviving driver of the Garve to Ullapool horse-drawn mail coaches. I don't know the frequency of the service, but staging points were at Altguish Inn and the Loch Droma (pronounced Loch Drome) homestead, the highest point of the route over the Dhirie More as it was called. There the weary horses were unhitched and fresh ones brought on. The Ullapool terminal for the service was what is still called 'The Old Arch Inn'. It was said that long after Charlie's transition to motor-powered transport, when he arrived at The Arch he would still audibly command his bus to 'whoa there'.

Snowstorms of that period seem to have been much heavier than nowadays. I recall a black and white 'snap' of Uncle Murdo sitting on the high roof of his Dodge limousine, his feet on the snow, *Altguish Inn* in the background.

I cannot vouch for the following story told me in my childhood of old Charlie, but probably true. Stuck in a violent snowstorm, his single passenger, a woman with a very young baby, he is said to have killed and disembowelled one of the horses, and put her and the baby inside it to preserve their lives. (I have heard a similar story from Canada, I think).

On reflection, Grandma Jane must have been a committed Christian, although I don't think her son and daughter at that time were. Nevertheless, we all adhered firmly to Grandma's perceived Christian routine. Our lives were governed by the daily round of morning and evening worship and Grace before meals. Also, depending on a specially devout and suitable 'Grace-sayer' being present, there would be Grace after meals as well.

For me at least life was pleasant if not idyllic. Sleeping quarters for Eva and me were in a wood-lined attic in Rosebank. We shared the room with Aunty Maggie. In winter, lighting was from a candle in a candlestick. Electric supply stopped on the floor below us, but even if it had reached our eyrie, we would still have been on candles, since the cost of electricity from the private village supply company was such that ordinary folk couldn't afford to use it. Even in the main living room, light was by a paraffin lamp. I well remember the outrage of the adults when there was a further price hike to one shilling per unit of electricity, and that was 5% of a reasonable worker's wage. An old age pension was 10/-, 50p today.

The house next door to Rosebank (now called Rosslynn) is a rebuild of the building of this period. It had at one time been an inn. Uncle Murdo had adapted the ground floor to make a cycle shop, where one could buy every part and many accessories for bicycles, also paraffin, petrol from a hand-operated pump out front at the street, methylated spirit, used for preheating pressure type paraffin lamps before lighting, but also drunk in the cities by penniless alcoholics. It was alcohol, but its consumption was a sure means of hastening the end of life, although that would not have been the intention of those who partook of it.

Out in the passage there was a heavy galvanised steel drum containing small chunks of carbide. This was used for bicycle lamps before battery operated ones came on stream. A carbide lamp had a small section at the bottom to contain the carbide and above that a small water reservoir with a screw type control valve. By opening the valve a drip feed of water fell on the carbide, which immediately gave off a highly inflammable gas. Apply a lit match to the gas jet, shut the hinged glass front and you were in business.

The former inn deserves a little further mention. Stairs, which had seen better days, ascended at one end giving access to the first floor and then on to a long divided attic above. There were two rooms on the first floor. From a small stairway landing, there was access to the first and major room. The plastered walls of this room looked like varnish finish on top of a dark fawn colour. It had unusual plasterwork, but the interesting feature was the three large murals of highland scenes, one on each of the un-windowed walls. My faded memory recalls one of a roaring stag and another a battle scene – Culloden? I'm sure that today, efforts would be made to preserve these pictures. The remaining wall was the one overlooking the street. Surprisingly for its time, it had a generous sized window. The whole must have been quite grand in its hey day. This room led into the other smaller room, but still of fair size.

As the tourist season came on, the large room became sleeping quarters for Eva and me, while Uncle Murdo was banished to the smaller room, thus releasing accommodation in Rosebank for the tourists. There was no running water in the former inn. Facilities for personal hygiene and natural needs consisted of a slop bucket, ewer (large jug) of water and basin and the other receptacle under the bed.

Three miles east of Ullapool stands Leckmelm, a mere handful of houses, but needing a small primary school, in the 1930s teachered by tall elegant, attractive and intelligent Miss Meg Macaulay. For years Uncle Murdo romanced Meg Macaulay, and for some mysterious reason it was a near unmentionable subject in our household and she never visited us. Nevertheless, night after night, Uncle Murdo, thoroughly spruced up, took off in his car and motored to Leckmelm. Usually the household was asleep before he returned.

And then, as for most children, there came the first big change away from the early innocence of childhood. Quite suddenly, it seemed to me, the day arrived when I had to go to school.

Ullapool, Wester Ross

Chapter 3

School Days

*A*unty Maggie had me on tow as we arrived for my first sight of the big green painted iron gates. There we met another lady, Mrs. Mahooah (really Mackenzie) with her wee boy Bertie, and for the next few years we were buddies. Bertie's later claim to fame came in WW2 when in the Royal Navy. He was ship's barber on a Royal Navy destroyer, the first ship into Tokyo bay at the Japanese surrender. Later he became, for a few years, the Ullapool village barber. Sadly, he died quite young.

Probably the worst feature of the infant class days was the wood framed slates and their accompanying slate pencils, with which we scratched and screeched our tedious way into the art of elementary writing and arithmetic. For a new page we held a little arm aloft and Miss Matheson quickly came with wet sponge on the end of a long stick, and swabbed down our efforts ready for a new start. If she was otherwise engaged, well, a good rub with the elbow of our woolly jersey sleeve, if necessary with a touch of spit added, did the job quite well. After all, if the sponge was on the wet side, the same sleeve probably had to do a bit of drying anyway.

When one had graduated to the dizzy heights of the third class in the room, now to a degree competent with paper and pencil, the ultimate reward for good performance was to be selected to take the sponge when it had become too dry, for wetting down in the nearby girls washroom. Curiously, our teacher was very deaf, which from her point of view, stuck all day in a large room full of little children was possibly something of a blessing.

Right through my school days, the absence of a pupil for a single day resulted in a home visit the same day from the school janitor to determine the reason. In earlier times, the caller was known as the 'Whipper In', or in more refined circles as the 'Attendance Inspector'. Nowadays, I often meet youngsters of very obvious school age, happily sauntering around our streets in twos and threes and usually smoking cigarettes. Nobody seems to bother. Our national laws have been so eroded and undermined that any person brave enough to interfere would probably land in court and quite possibly prison – I think it's called 'post-modern progress'.

My school progress was made to the next room, classes two and three, a year in each, under the strict jurisdiction of a powerful lady known to us as Tina Bull, who was given to expressing her displeasure with a formidable on the spot stamp of her substantial shoe. It says a lot for the quality of our recently built school building, and perhaps in part explains the need for it. I cannot leave this lady Tina, really Miss Mackenzie without recording the following: Tina added to her income by running a well-stocked sweet and paper shop. One, Duncan, a year or two my senior, but at this time still unable to see over the counter and with something of a childish lisp in speech had somehow managed to gain possession of a penny, (wealth indeed). He is said to have gone into the shop and asked for 'a pennyworth of black thriped ballth' to which the good lady had to say, "I'm sorry Duncan, I'm out of them." From her eager customer came the swift response, "Lieth, I'm thmelling them."

* * *

In the summer of 1932 Papa arrived in Ullapool for his one and only holiday back to Europe in his lifetime. The yoyo toy had made its first appearance in Ullapool and Eva and I received one each, brightly coloured, red one side, green the other. It was beautiful weather, and banished to the attic at bedtime, we were desperate to use them. For some reason, I tried to use mine out the attic window and down the steeply sloping slate roof. Suddenly I lost hold of the string. Yoyo and string landed in the roof gutter at the bottom of the slates.

In some apprehension of adult rebuke, I felt urgency to retrieve it. In my wisdom of six summers, the solution seemed to be to go out the window and reach down for it. At first go, I found the slates so hot from the day's sun that I had to retreat and spread my dressing gown on the slates. I was very conscious of the men of the village 'parliament' gathered for their evening blether at the village clock which at that time stood in the middle of the street at the top of the Quay Lane. I did not want to be discovered and I was concerned about the drop from the gutter to the concrete path and garden below. Clutching anxiously with one hand to the window frame and pressing flat as I could to the slates, I still failed to make it. My precious yoyo remained in the gutter overnight. Next day, perhaps it was Eva who made Papa aware of my trouble. He came up for a look, fetched a long handled umbrella and in no time flipped the yoyo down to the garden below – sighs of childish relief. The rest of the household heard nothing about it.

* * *

In due course primary classes were left behind, and my class entered the exalted heights of higher grade. To the tiddlers of primaries, we became beings of some status. History, Geography, Mathematics, Latin, French, not even the adults at home knew about this stuff, or so we tended to think.

The whole system was ruthlessly governed by a headmaster armed with a nasty 'Lochgelly' leather strap, an application of which could bring the colour to one's cheeks. My memory will never die of the horrendous occasion when he tried to exercise his discipline on 'Inga Jane', a lad a little older than myself, and he at last met his match. For some unknown reason, Inga had decided that singing in the music class was not for him. The top man was sent for; Inga was marched outside into the corridor, and we heard the sobering sound of six of the 'Lochgelly best' being brought down on his bare outstretched hands. Believe me our man was powerful and spared nothing when he applied his weapon, I know because I've experienced it for some 'misdemeanour' with a stink bomb. Inga returned to the class, but no change had been brought about. A further five times the punishment was meted out and still no change except now, blood was amply evident on Inga's hands. He still did not sing, nor did he shed a tear. There wasn't much of him, but I really admired him that day, as did many others. The music teacher was in tears; Inga's face was slightly reddened and the master disciplinarian retired defeated. There the matter ended, with not even a parental complaint. Unless you had considerable clout, you didn't in those days.

Came the Second World War – at the age of nineteen, valiant Inga became a Sergeant in the British army. Like many of his generation he has now passed on.

* * *

Fortunately life did have lighter moments. After breaks, pupils were summoned back to the grind with the loud ringing of a hand-bell. We boys lined up in three rows facing the steps leading to our door and the duty teacher appeared to march us indoors. On one memorable occasion, his appearance was swiftly followed by Mr. Headmaster who immediately took over the parade and in his crisp military manner announced, "John Mackay, come here, my boy."

The atmosphere was tense. Mr. H. shot down the steps, confronted John, took hold of his zip slider and, virtually in one movement, whipped it down while with his free hand plucked out into view a large dead rabbit. The scene would have done credit to a conjuror.

Nevertheless, he, the rabbit and John disappeared indoors and I never did hear if the Lochgelly was exercised. Obviously, John had been spotted checking a rabbit snare during his break, really I think more to be commended than rebuked. In World War Two, John became a paratrooper and if there were rabbits around, he and his mates would not have gone hungry.

A variety of teachers, male, female, bright, dull, interesting, amusing, contributed to our learning before each went their way, some to military service, and one thereby to his death.

During schooldays a number of changes took place in my life. As each long year came and went, new delights were discovered. There was fishing for cuddies (baby fish) under the pier, then growing bolder, out of sight of adults, at low tide making our careful way about the pier under-structure and observing the creatures who lived below going about their business, little fish, crabs and lobsters. There was an old friend of Papa's, one Billy Obb, a former trawler man who trawled in the days when it really was a tough and hazardous occupation. Billy had a sturdy rowing-cum-sail boat with which he did a bit of fishing in the deep water of Loch Broom. He could earn a few shillings selling his catches to the local hotels. Having set his long lines with a row of baited hooks attached he would return, weather permitting 24 hours later to claim his reward and put new bait on the hooks. The process was made easier by a second person to man the oars and keep moving the boat along, and sometimes I was the lucky lad picked for the job. My 'pay' was a sizeable fish from the mixed catch of cod, haddock, ling, skate and others. I could present my fish at home with some pride; I've since learned that pride is not a good thing. Now, there are no fish in the loch, having been swept clean by illegal trawling, which our hapless authorities did nothing about.

Uncle Murdo bought, I think for £8, a second hand neat brown, varnished rowing boat. My pals and I enjoyed many a leisurely summer evening, exploring the rocky eastern fringe of Loch Broom. Not one of us could swim, nor had we life jackets. In those days they had scarcely been heard of. On one occasion, we even achieved a third place (against adults) in the only rowing race I ever experienced in Ullapool.

* * *

With the arrival of WW2, there came also a large fleet of steam and a few motor drift net fishing vessels. These hailed mostly from the Scottish east coast fishing ports, Buckie, Fraserburgh, Peterhead, and Aberdeen. The move of course was inspired because of the vulnerability to enemy action of their peacetime home ports and fishing grounds. Their move was probably obligatory by Government regulation. The strange 'foreign' Doric dialect of the crews was fascinating. As school boys we soon made friends, mastered the language, scrambled about their boats and were introduced to a new fishing lure, various brightly coloured fly hooks, six or eight of them strung out along a single piece of line gut and ending with a lead sinker. These were highly effective among the abundance of mackerel in the loch.

Trailed astern of the rowing boat, or simply swung out from the pier or drifter's side, one could haul them in six at a time. The previously largely undisturbed herring shoals of the Minch and west sea lochs provided a lucrative livelihood for most of the new arrivals. I have seen them carefully approaching their pier berths, with decks just about awash with the weight of their catches. On a Saturday, after discharging their catches, the crews, normally nine or ten rotund figures tried to get home to the east coast for the weekend, putting to sea again on Monday afternoon.

The majority of the men were staunch and sincere Christians. War or no war, they would never sail or fish on a Sunday. Quite often skippers, when going home for a weekend, would anchor their ships out in the loch. One or two of them cottoned on to the usefulness of 'my' little brown rowing boat for ferrying them ashore.

It was on such an occasion on a day of strong wind and big waves that I was roped in for the job. I had some apprehension about the conditions, but in my early teens, I didn't argue with mature experienced men of the sea – their young men were all away on war service. Alongside their vessel, my dinghy was behaving like a bucking bronco, but as each blue suited heavy weight stepped in, it gradually steadied and settled lower and lower in the water, till with heart in mouth, I started rowing for shore with my ten imperturbable passengers. The dinghy's freeboard was dangerously deficient, each wave liberally spraying the crew, but it didn't seem to bother them in the slightest. With relief we safely made it to shore.

Perhaps here I may record little incidents bypassed on my way. I was aged, I think, about twelve when somewhat to my surprise I was invited to join three of my contemporaries who had somehow acquired a packet of twenty *Craven A* cigarettes. On a sunny summer afternoon, we settled down behind a suitable screen of gorse bushes part way up the Ullapool hill and lit up – high adventure. At one sitting, we polished off the whole packet and by a miracle, not one of us was sick, nor detected by our respective family adults.

In the upper part of Loch Broom, at Ardnaluchd (local pronunciation 'Ardnalou'), there was a sizeable wooden pier which had been specially built for the shipping of timber from the Braemore forest. The pier almost certainly dated back to the 1914-18 era when timber would have been in high demand. I've heard the previous generation speak of the work being carried out by German prisoners of war.

In the course of my life, I witnessed the growth and felling of three timber harvests from the same Braemore ground. Sometime, in the mid-thirties after a wild overnight storm, and having just wakened, I peered out the bedroom window and was amazed to see a large squarish object drifting through the Loch Broom narrows and heading slowly towards Ullapool. It turned out to be half the Ardnalou pier, riding high and smoothly in the calm after the storm. It kept the more enterprising of the natives warm, burning in their fireplaces for many a day thereafter.

* * *

From an early age, I was becoming familiar with motor vehicles. Uncle Murdo had a small contract for each Saturday in summer when the two Rose brothers of lime juice fame were in residence at their respective shooting lodges on their Rhiddoroch estates just north of Ullapool. The first was four miles up the glen and the next, four miles further on. One lived on his own, the other may have had a wife with him, but I suspect not. They each had a retinue of servants, including cooks, waitresses, housemaids, gardeners, chauffeurs, gamekeepers and ghillies as required, first class vehicles, large fishing loch and salmon rivers. Nevertheless it was necessary to hire Murdo's car to deliver the weekly supplies and Saturday mail, not to mention large laundry hampers from Annabella Chalan (Annabel Colin).

Annabella lived with her tall, gangling brother Willie in their two-attic accommodation, on Pultney Street, and week by week, she turned out hampers of immaculately laundered white sheets, shirts etc, drawing water in pails from a street supply, heating it and her irons over their one coal fire, probably for modest reward.

Once a year, Murdo's car brought back to the village, from the Roses, an assortment of portions of venison, haunches, etc. of deer, for nominated persons, some rich, some poor. There was always a piece for Annabella.

One of the brothers had a thing about speed, not fast but the opposite. Very occasionally, he made the 60-mile journey to Inverness in his very capable car. His chauffeur was under strict instruction not to exceed 15 mph. The passenger always sat in the rear left seat. There were two advantages; it helped to balance the car, and more importantly he could observe the speedometer. When in the heat of a summer day, the chauffeur's attention strayed during the four-hour journey and the speedo' needle strayed upward into forbidden territory, the chauffeur would receive an immediate tap on his shoulder, and the curt reminder that 'there is no hurry'.

I was always allowed to accompany Murdo's driver on the regular Saturday Rhiddoroch jaunts. Usually they were good for a delicious jammy scone or other tasty bite from the cook, and thus I spent my driving apprenticeship on the single track, very narrow gravel surfaced road, bordered with deep open drains for the abundant surface water. The drains were also very effective vehicle traps for the novice or untutored. Once, I had to be rescued when in early days I had ditched. I was driving a small *Bedford* truck, and the road breadth gave just about zero leeway. It made for a high standard of driving accuracy.

By the age of fourteen, I was doing the Saturday Rhiddoroch run regularly, and unaccompanied. Once I started driving, I never had a tutor driver with me. I had learned mainly by observing how my elders had gone about it, and with entirely voluntary help from one or two amazingly trusting adults, not least of which was our village policeman; strange behaviour for the appointed upholder of the law. Oddly enough, some sixty years later, a lady in conversation with me mentioned the gentleman's name, and on learning that I had known him, asked me if I could possibly write down what I knew, for the benefit of his son. What follows is the result:

Memories of P.C. Jim Munro (Surely Surely)

Jim Munro, his wife and daughter Margaret came to Ullapool as far as I can recall, around 1936, when I was 10 years old. At that time, Ullapool was a quiet Highland village of about 500 population. Departed memory cells limit the accuracy of this account sixty-odd years later, but in the words of an old Irish acquaintance, 'it will be near enough'.

Our back yard bordered onto the vegetable garden of the village policeman. Consequently, one was in fairly close touch with affairs at the police station, a traditional two-storey house with a two-room cell block tacked onto its rear. It was always intriguing to speculate what lay behind the high steel grilled windows. The house still stands and is now a private residence. Prior to Jim's arrival, the village had been policed by a quiet retiring man, Thomson Mackenzie, who after a long illness died, more or less in harness.

The community mourned his passing, as did his widow and five children. In those days, policemen were scantily paid; police work was mostly routine stuff, the odd form, checks on gun licenses etc.

The shutting of public bars at the mandatory hours of 3 p.m. and 9 p.m. entailed a token appearance of the constable.

Jim Munro, as our new constable, came with a breath of fresh air to the village – young, lean, fit, of a lively disposition and a brilliant whistler, who could often be heard even when not seen. He had been a blacksmith prior to joining the police. He was extremely fit and agile. I recall seeing him perform a 'party trick' with a sledge-hammer wielded single-handed. He challenged those present, but no one could repeat it. Later, as a young man, I had a go myself and came close to permanently damaging my wrist.

Jim was a frequent caller at my uncle's garage on Pultney St., where my informal mechanical apprenticeship was getting off the ground from an early age. Jim's calls were of a purely social nature and many an interesting bit of gossip I lugged into. Serious police work must have been minimal, the main sleuthing centring on dastardly acts on Halloween night.

These idyllic days pre-1939 and pre-Second World War rapidly changed with its coming. Navy crews from visiting ships and a large contingent of lumbermen from British Honduras livened up the scene and occasionally clashed with violence.

1940 – I was still in school when the first invasion alert occurred. The sight of a cycling messenger popping a couple of 'Molotov Cocktails' (petrol bombs) over the school fence for an older lad, a member of 'Dad's Army', speeded my pulse rate. At 14, I couldn't make it for enlistment, but I was called on to man the 'nerve centre' at the *Caledonian Hotel* telephone.

The villages bevy of 1914-18 veterans and even a couple with Boer War service frequented their favourite 'watering' holes and put the world and the war to rights. The east coast fishing fleet crews brought a further population influx of fishermen, salesmen, buyers, lorry drivers and others. Jim's empire took on deep change and probably required for him, increased relaxation to counteract the new stresses. He sometimes found it provident to see to the closing of the public bars by doing so from the inside, having first ushered out those not familiar with the rules of the game. His cronies having earlier retired to the 'Gents' would then emerge for the serious work of the evening; the camaraderie must have been marvellous. The 'West' had its own interpretation of the laws of the land and it worked very well.

In the 1930s, car ownership was not common among ordinary folk, neither were policemen well paid, but somehow Jim achieved ownership of a neat dark blue *Austin 10*.

My Uncle Murdo ran a small country garage in the village – petrol, puncture repairs, a five-ton truck and a hire car. Among the village characters was one Coineachan, better known as the Duke. The Duke had a '1914' arm and shoulder full of repair pins, plates and screws. The arm itself operated by a system of leather straps round his body and hooked up to the other arm. He chain smoked cigarettes and kept his system running with a plentiful intake of whisky. Now, in the year 1940 it happened that the Duke, a bachelor, was laid low with an attack of gout.

Uncle Murdo, seeing me arrive home from school (aged 14), despatched me with his large hiring car with a gift to the Duke, probably a book, or some delicacy for his evening meal. Answering the Duke's shouted 'come in', I guess I must have been speechless to behold sitting at the patient's bedside, Jim Munro – uniformed!

"Got you, you little b-------," he said, "so, you're driving... well, for that, you can drive me home'.

Taking his leave of the Duke, he installed himself in the back seat, behind the partition sliding window of the *Austin* and I, his 14-year-old chauffeur, full of wonder and some trepidation, drove him in state to the police station. As he left the car, he turned to me and said, "Tell your uncle you're a better driver than he is and tell him I said it."

Of course, I didn't. Don't make waves where none are necessary.

* * *

Several times, Murdo unable to meet his transport commitments in those early war years, sent me to borrow Jim's *Austin 10*, which was readily handed over, but with warnings – one time, "Mind that back tyre," through which the inner tube was visibly protruding. Another time it was, "Be careful now, it's not insured you know'. In spite of these minor impediments, my journeys passed uneventfully. By the time I was 16, with Jim's full approval, I was driving fish trucks from Ullapool to Aberdeen, return – a round trip of just under 330 miles.

Black out driving was something else! Light from a single masked headlight was minimal. Several times, disaster was narrowly averted, once as I almost ran into the tail end of an unlit farm tractor and trailer making its leisurely way on the east coast roads. Part of the wartime vehicle lighting regulations required that by applying a halfpenny to it, a vehicle sidelight must be completely blacked out. In the hours of darkness, if Jim had had a minor celebration, he was known to apply his legal halfpenny to the many visiting trucks loading fish at the pier. He was simply going through the motions and all concerned left it at that. Jim was a practical and popular policeman.

The news broke that Jim was to be transferred to the village of Dornie. Ullapool waited in some apprehension for his successor. I can only say Ullapool's loss was Dornie's gain.

P.S. Jim's standard conversational response was a crisp 'surely surely'...and thus he was known.

Recently, I received as a present from my good wife – a mobile phone, a complication to life, which up till then I had managed to avoid. Now, having wrestled successfully with at least some of its mysteries, I am starting to appreciate its merits. As I reflect on telephones, or essentially their technology progress that now seems to be racing ahead virtually uncontrollably, my mind boggles as I recall in the early 1930s the installation of Uncle

Murdo's first telephone in Rosebank. It was in the entrance hall, a large, stained wooden box screwed to the wall at stand up height. Its number was 'Ullapool 7', just one digit, which has by now become last of a string of ten digits to make the same connection, and apparently without the involvement of any other human being. The majority of village numbers were single digit, although one or two probably scraped up to two digits. To make a call, one picked up the heavy earpiece (the mouthpiece remained attached to the wooden box) and gave the little cranked handle at the side a couple of turns to alert the exchange.

The telephone exchange was installed in an ordinary domestic dwelling house on Pultney St. It was manned by the residents, Kenny 'Sailor' and his wife. Later, it was moved to No.9, Ladysmith Street, Mr. and Mrs. Macdonald, universally known as Kenny and Kate Deedilan.

Whence the name Deedilan?

In Ullapool, I suppose as elsewhere, it was a common practice to deal with a fretful infant by singing to it a lively little tune while bouncing it up and down on one's knee. The treatment and, separately, the music were known as 'deedling'. Old Kenny was a lifelong singer of Gaelic songs, and much given to 'deedling' them. Hence, he was known as The Deedlan.

In his capacity as exchange operator, he found a ready-made captive audience, while he went through the often lengthy business of completing his callers' required connections. It may be that, on occasions, his extensive repertoire contributed to the waiting times.

Now, in stark contrast, I pick up my recently acquired 'mobile', press one pre-programmed button and in the twinkling of an eye, my call is shot up to some satellite and bounced back to earth to my desired contact, almost anywhere. Despite all the time saved, I seem to have less of it than ever. No doubt that is in some measure due to the very reduced rate of action brought about by the latter end of a lifetime.

I suppose I could ramble on a long time about Ullapool's characters and worthies. Most had survived the trauma of the 1914-18 trenches, and one or two the Boer War. Few of them were known by their real names, but often had some affectionate nickname. To name but a few, there was 'Starkey', carpenter, undertaker, and keen beekeeper, his brother 'Rajah', retired from building railways in India. There was a tailor, Johnnie 'Calamity' who spent most days hand-line fishing from a boat with the Rajah; 'the Bird', painter and decorator par excellence, and his mock enemy 'the Skate', skilled motor mechanic. Thereby hang a few little tales.

On a pleasant day, the Bird was going about his business high on the roof of what is now the harbour office, although my first memory of it was as a motor garage. As the Skate was heading homeward for lunch, the heavens opened up and down came the rain in torrents, a not unusual event in Ullapool. The Bird making for his ladder and terra firma and noticing his pal, shouted down a greeting, "It's a fine day for skates." Quick on the draw, the Skate grabbed and removed the ladder, shouting back, "Aye, and you can fly down Bird," leaving his feathered friend stranded and very wet till after lunch.

Neither the Bird's superior age nor his Boer War years spared him the banter of his contemporaries. One day, as he was busily painting the inside of our first (and red) telephone kiosk, Starkey happening along, paused to weigh up this new contrivance in the village, then loudly uttered, "Well, well, Alex, they got a cage for you at last."

Both Starkey and Skate were keen beekeepers. Skate had a wicked sense of humour and he was completely immune to bee stings. He never wore any kind of protection when working with bees. As he pulled honey-laden frames and sections from a hive, he would brush the bees from it with his bare hands. He thought it a great joke to reach into the hive, scoop up a handful of bees and throw them at you.

One time, he bought a new swarm of special Italian bees. Shortly afterwards, Starkey was observed one day sitting on a box in front of one of his hives and with a hammer in his hand. Every now and then, the hammer came down smartly on the entrance platform to the hive.

An intrigued passer-by stopped to ask what was going on. The reply came, "I'm killing these damn Italians of Skate's; they're robbing my hive." Italians, under their dictator Benito Mussolini having not long before invaded Ethiopia, were not much in favour anyway.

Then there was the wonderful tale of the 'Lady with a Leak'. A certain Mr. Macleod, proprietor of the Pier Garage (now harbour offices) was called from this life at an early age. In the early thirties, his widow, best known as Mrs. Ena, her two sons still schoolboys, bravely continued to run the establishment, ably assisted by the earlier referred to, Skate.

One day a lady, full of airs and graces, and dressed accordingly, came into Mrs. Ena's office via the street door. With a mouth full of marbles, she made it known that her car radiator had developed a serious leak and she needed it repaired. With quick assessment of her would-be customer, Mrs Ena opened the door leading into the garage and addressed her head mechanic, slowly, loudly and very clearly, "Alex, there's a lady here with a leak." There followed some levelling out of social status.

I suppose one good tale deserves another. In my childhood, when supermarkets hadn't even been dreamed of, I was often required to pop down to our local shop and purchase some household item that was running low. Thus did I learn of 'Dol Gordon's jam'. When toilet rolls first came on stream as a new item of stock they were naturally on prominent display. From Dol Gordon's garb, he was almost certainly an old man who had spent a lot of his life involved with the sea. On an occasion while doing some shopping, he noticed these round packages on the shelf behind the counter. Having made his other purchases, his appetite whetted and his eyes now probably not as sharp as they once were, he added, "And I'll have a pot of that jam." Thereafter, for many a day, the now essential rolls were referred to as 'Dol Gordon's jam'. Many of the village population economised, simply by cutting up the daily newspaper (price, one old penny) and saved on loo 'jam'!

In our early teens, there was one among us who had better remain nameless. From the first road bridge on the Garve road, there was a wonderful outlook over steeply falling ground and over Loch Broom. At a considerable distance, halfway down the hill, marched the row of poles carrying the main telephone wires, each one anchored to the pole cross bars on a white porcelain insulator. The 'one', being a country loon, was skilled in hunting and the use of missiles – in this case, simply stones from the roadside. With these, from the bridge, he could pick off these insulators at will and never miss. The insulators immediately shattering to fragments – an impressive although not commendable skill!

Like in most stories, there has to be some less pleasant memories, and an important one of these was that at some stage in my boyhood, Aunty Maggie became seriously ill. It was an unnamed illness from which she never properly recovered. For Eva and me, it made a radical change for she had in effect become our surrogate mother. At the time, we were aged about 14 and 10 respectively. Maggie was laid up on the ground floor sitting room divan. From the sparse information being passed to us, it appeared that there was a distinct likelihood she would die.

While we mainly fended for ourselves as best we could, over a long period she made a halting recovery of sorts, but never again took any great interest in anything except her Bible, church services and Uncle Murdo's new and first baby, Seonaid, whom she liked to take for pram walks.

At some stage, Eva, who was really an intellectual, departed to Edinburgh University, but within a year threw up the traces and got herself a secretarial job in Glasgow. She never came back to Ullapool until well after the deaths of Maggie and Grandma Jane, nor did she communicate with them. I, myself, still a schoolboy, was left in a somewhat dependant and uncomfortable position in the Ullapool household. The adults were highly displeased at Eva's abandoning of her academic career. Papa's financial support of his family had fizzled out due to a drastic slump in the Argentinian economy.

As mentioned earlier, in 1932, when I was 6 years old, he had visited Mama in Germany and came for a holiday to Ullapool. Although to myself he was almost a complete stranger, on the first morning after his arrival Eva and I shyly entered his bedroom and crept into bed, one on each side of him. He was heavily tanned and he had the pleasant smell of the pure tobacco of those days. With an arm about each of us, he joked and taught us little endearments in Spanish, the language of his Patagonia. It was the one occasion in my life I was consciously close to him. All too soon, it was over and Uncle Murdo drove him the full way to Liverpool and the ship taking him back to 'the far country'. I never saw him again. Uncle Murdo's motor journey in itself was no mean undertaking in those days.

Later in life, my old friend Billy Obb, who was a contemporary and former pal of Papa's, told me it had been Papa's intention to have a further 3 years in Patagonia and then start up a business in Ullapool. It was never to be, the well known words of our national poet concerning the 'best laid schemes of mice and men' echoed God's Biblical advice about the laying of plans, materialising in the ensuing Argentinian economic collapse. Aged 64, Papa passed away and was laid to rest in a cemetery in Puerto Natales, the town of my birth.

Some years later, Manolo, the seafaring youngest member of the Maclean family saw the grave when visiting that of his own Dad. Years afterwards I learned snippets about Papa here and there. He had had a great yearning on his visit home to return to his mother's family home in Strath Kanaird and sleep, even once, wrapped up in the homely smell of the 'crottle' (home dyed) blankets of his early years.

Thankfully, this he managed to do – the house, *Rose Cottage*, still stands by the roadside at the top of Strath Kanaird brae and is occupied to this day. It appears that during his stay, he volunteered to take the collie dog to the hill and bring home the three or four croft cows for milking. In his enthusiasm, forgetting himself, and probably using the methods of the pampas, the docile Strath Kanaird cows got such a rude awakening that they were seen charging down the hillside, and leaping the croft fence in there rush to escape from him.

My senior cousin Johnie Ceylon (Macdonald) at that time ran a smallholding in the Black Isle. For reasons unknown, it was called Ceylon and so was he. Ceylon was a fiery little man with a sweet wife and daughter, also two teenage sons. Papa paid them a visit and later, Simon, the elder son, told me about it, and his high regard for Papa's skills.

It happened on a day when Ceylon was temporarily off the premises; the lads had been left to sort out some of the precious sheep stock when one of the animals went into a bog. They couldn't get it out – crises situation. If Ceylon should return he would at the very least, blow his top. Papa happened onto the scene, took control, and issued his order, "Get me a rope, son."

The rope was produced in double quick time, swiftly fashioned into a lasso, whirled in the air and deftly placed over the nearly-lost sheep, which was then hauled to firm ground. Sighs of relief.

Ceylon himself had been through the mill in his younger days. One day in his later life, I was sympathising with him in Strath Kanaird, as together we watched a flash flood sweeping his meagre corn harvest down the river. In crisp tones, he quickly put me right in respect of the unseasonable torrential rain, "Look here, boy, we're bad with it, but we'd be a lot worse without it!"

He then told me of his days shepherding in North America. They entailed driving sheep across some notorious desert. He said there had been occasions when he'd had to cut a button from his clothing to suck and try to induce moisture in his mouth. He also told me of a night sitting with others round their campfire when a heavily bearded stranger rode in on a great black horse with, as Ceylon described it, enough silver on it for King George. The man asked which one was John Macdonald (Ceylon), then introduced himself as a relative from Strath Kanaird. After some hospitality and a chat, the bandit, (for such he was), like the Lone Ranger rode off into the sunset and they never met again.

I recall Ceylon inviting me to the *Caledonian Hotel* bar for a quick dram. Two glasses of whisky promptly arrived on the high counter. My enquiry whether he would like a splash of water in his, drew the immediate response, "Certainly, certainly, boy, if it wasn't for the water, I'd be dead years ago'.

Chapter 4

Transition to Adult Life

*F*or some, the transition to adulthood arrives long before its logical time, and to some extent that was how it came upon me. From early days I was captivated with motor vehicles. Uncle Murdo with his new wife was installed in his rebuilt house, the one-time inn. Transport business was starting to come to life. His wife Meg, prior to the arrival of a family, still taught at Leckmelm some three miles away. There was a war on; everything was scarce, not least money. They had bought a very second hand, and probably more hands, *Austin 7*, popularly known as a *'Baby' Austin*. Its essential purpose was to ferry Meg to and from her job. I was only too happy to become useful by doing the driving.

Already in my last months at school, Uncle M was using me to drive his *Austin* truck fully laden with 5 tons of flour from Ullapool to the railway at Garve station some 30 miles away.

Uncle M seemed to have a strong distaste for physical work of any kind, (perhaps he was unwell), thus he would have the flour loaded during the day and the truck ready for departure immediately on my arrival home from school. My buddy Edwin Pirie usually accompanied me on these trips – for us, high adventure, and we relished heaving the 140lbs (65kgs) bags and stowing them in the rail vans.

A few times on a Saturday, I was sent to Garve for a load of barrels of bitumen, used for road repairs. These weighed approximately 5cwt each (250kgs), 20 of them made a load.

I soon learned the art of moving them single-handed from rail to road truck, an impossible sounding feat for a stripling of a youth, but I assure you not so. Standing upright, the wooden barrels were curved over their height, tip them onto their side and they rolled easily from truck to truck, then using the barrel's curve and its own momentum, tip it upright again, making sure it would

51

land on the right spot. Five tons loaded in about half-an-hour and I would feel like the Biblical horse in the book of Job, 'rejoicing in his strength'; but it wasn't strength so much as technique. Later in my life in the construction industry, the lessons learned stood me in good stead as I manhandled barrels of oil, bulldozer tracks and weighty parts, often with little or no assistance.

Vehicle driving tests had been suspended in the War years, and when I became 16, I was eligible to legally hold a driving licence and did so for the next 60 years without ever having had a test. I have to confess I had grown to hate school and particularly its headmaster. At the age of sixteen, I simply stopped going and nobody appeared to object. Aunty Maggie was semi-invalid; she took little interest in anything other than sitting by the old kitchen range fireside reading her Bible.

To help the war effort, the British government in its 'wisdom' brought a contingent of native British Hondurans to fell the Leckmelm woods. A hutted camp and sawmill were quickly established for them where *Tir-Aluinn* house is now, although it wasn't called that in those days. Black and coffee coloureds were something of a novelty in Ullapool. Long before the era of political correctness, one old man referred to them as the 'darks', probably his abbreviation for the word we mustn't mention now. The 'darks' took very badly to our west highland climate, many of them succumbed to flus, bronchial troubles, etc. To come to town (Ullapool), they often hired Murdo's *Baby Austin*, and I would ferry them in for the handsome fare of a shilling (5p) a head. I was given the task of teaching one of them to read and write, and paid a pittance for it. Probably enough, as my efforts were a distinct failure!

Nevertheless, they brought some benefits in the form of tree backs, or 'slabs' as we called them, by-products of the sawmill. These were in demand by the 'Ullapudlians' for firewood at 30 shillings (£1.50) a load, a real bargain against the high price of coal, which was often of poor quality. I hauled stacks of them with the *Austin* truck. I was extra keen to do the job on a Saturday, because there was the bonus of a free evening film show at the camp. There were of course no films in Ullapool, although later, an organisation called the Highlands & Islands Film Guild introduced an intermittent service with a touring van.

Occasionally, a consignment of Jamaican rum arrived for the timber men. It had the effect of sending some of them berserk. One Saturday night as I came to the main building to pay for my load of slabs, there was a running battle in progress and some of them were, in deadly earnest, chasing others through the trees brandishing long lopping knives and machêtes. I hurried with low profile to Major Smith's office to pay my bill and found him at work, with a pistol on his desk.

In the War years, motorcar tyres were near to unobtainable. It was common to see vehicles, private and commercial, running with the rubber tyre tread completely worn away, and large areas of the white and final inner canvas layer being presented to the none-too smooth road surfaces. So it was at the birth of Murdo's first child, a girl, Seonaid (Jessie) in Inverness. He got me to drive him there with the *Baby Austin* for his first fatherly visit. In the event, our second tyre puncture occurred a few miles west of *Altguish Inn* and he had to leave me. He hitched a lift with the first east-bound lorry that came along. Unfortunately, its cab was already full. It was cold weather and the last I saw of him he was sitting on bare boards of the rear platform, hands deep in pockets and crouching as low as possible into his overcoat. For myself, I managed to patch up one tyre sufficiently to trundle back home.

At 16 years of age, 'Dad's Army' relented and accepted me into their ranks. At its start-up, all it had was men past the age for military service – no uniforms, no weapons. A government source recommended that they arm themselves with staffs or staves to ward off the threatened arrival of the mighty German war machine. Whitehall didn't seem to realise that there was a limit even to the British sense of humour.

Fortunately in the Highlands, the local estate owners rallied round and handed over their very good quality hunting firearms and the ammunition to go with them. Uncle M fell heir to a lovely little 0.22 rifle, the property of Lady Fowler of Braemore, whose late husband Sir John was of some fame locally as one of the engineers responsible for the construction of the Forth rail bridge. The village clock still stands to his memory.

A few mornings later, Uncle M and I rose early, and drove up to Morefield to try out the new toy on the profusion of local rabbits. Fortunately for the rabbits, we didn't get a single hit.

By the time of my enlistment, the original title of 'Local Defence Volunteers' had been changed to the tidier 'Home Guard'. They were now equipped with khaki battle-dress uniforms, great coats, hats, 'tin' hats, and boots. There were sturdy old, but accurate, *Ross* rifles with detachable bayonets, and eventually *Sten* guns and one beast of an automatic rifle, which I was required to bear. I say 'beast' because of its great weight, and although automatic, its magazine only held ten rounds. We had lots of training sessions in the local Territorial Drill Hall.

When Italy entered the war on the side of the Germans, their main forces mustered in North Africa, aimed at threatening the British presence in Egypt and eastward, the vital Suez Canal. Their General Officer Commanding, if I remember correctly, was one Marshal Graziani. This gentleman had a stubbly grey beard and hairy visage. The Brits quickly dubbed him 'Electric Whiskers'.

About the same time there came on our scene a new training officer who could readily have doubled for Graziani. This poor man seemed to suffer from shell shock and old wound injuries, from which war we couldn't tell. As he demonstrated various methods of silent attack and despatch of enemy sentries, etc., various parts of him tended to shake and tremble. Naturally, he quickly became our very own 'Electric Whiskers'.

Soon after my arrival, Uncle M dropped out of parade attendances. The old boys had already had war up to their ears,

54

but we teenagers enjoyed the excitement of playing at soldiers. We had plenty fun charging about the hillsides, dropping into cover and firing at practice targets on butts up the Rhiddoroch road. There was a mock invasion carried out by regular army commandoes down Gruinard way. Having never seen *Sten* guns they were amazed to see Dad's Army with them. One of these hardy army men was captured by, or perhaps in the hope of an easy time, gave himself up to a gamekeeper, whose old female employer promptly had him locked in a cellar where she kept him for three days on bread and water.

Somewhere along the line, an RAF recruiting van appeared in the village and I volunteered for aircrew service, was called to Doncaster for medical examination, but that was the last I heard of it. Only much later, I learned that, without my knowledge, I had already been designated as being on essential service – hauling fish, etc. towards the war effort. Probably, that's one of the reasons I'm alive today, aircrew service was considered exciting but often of short duration.

As Uncle Murdo's children came along, in anticipation of baptism or 'Christening' as they called it, he started attending church again. He agonised, learning parrot fashion, the Shorter Catechism, based on the Westminster Confession of Faith a knowledge of which was a requirement for parents seeking baptism in the Free Presbyterian Church of Scotland, which his parents Lachlan and Grandma Jane had probably attended from its inception

At some point between teen's and adulthood, I myself got to wondering about God and the Bible. Did God really exist? Was the Bible significantly true? Over a period, these thoughts at intervals popped into my head. None of my contemporaries appeared to give the matter a moment's thought. The generation immediately before me simply didn't discuss the matter. Some attended church some didn't, but for Grandma Jane's generation it was different – regular church going, morning and night, family worship with Bible reading and her prayers in Gaelic. We all went on our knees A.M. and P.M. Daily. Eva and I were required to read aloud alternately (in English) through a chapter at each session. Weekly Sunday school was a must; in fact it was the one break we as children had from the strict rules of the Presbyterian 'Sabbath' – indoors all day, quiet, no toys, no playing games, no music or singing, none but 'good' books to be read.

While Auntie Maggie was in health there was always an excellent main meal after the 'morning' service, which perhaps curiously to the uninitiated, started at noon. I think the reason for that was to accommodate the feeding of livestock and the arrival thereafter of country dwellers.

The services, with stern sermons, I might say were never less than two hours and often a good bit longer. For children, the one break in the tedium of the day was to leave home as early as possible to relax with our fellows before the Sunday school teacher made his appearance. He was Angus Macleod, a carpenter, and in hindsight, a man of God if ever there was one. Day school included Bible class from infants through to the end. Through it all I acquired a fair knowledge of the Bible in spite of my inclinations for the world. I didn't realise it at the time, but again in hindsight I have become very conscious of the privilege that was mine in having such Christian influences in my younger days.

Eventually the mental questions of God and the Bible bothered me sufficiently to cause me to start reading 'The Book'. It has been said that the famous Scottish writer Sir Walter Scott when on his deathbed asked his son Lockart to bring the book. Perhaps a little naïve, Lockart inquired, "Which book, father?" The old man put him right, with the words, "Lockart, there is only one book." I found The Book very interesting and when I came to the Gospels and read of the crucifixion of Jesus Christ, I was overcome with emotion and wept. Although it did not make a great difference in my life for many years, I knew I was reading truth.

Uncle Murdo had got a contract with an Aberdeen fish merchant for the haulage of herring from the heavy local landings to

Aberdeen. He started taking me with him on his journeys. Usually it was late afternoon before the journey started; in winter, often in darkness. Before long I was doing it alone. The cab interior was bare metal and of course there was no cab heater. The Home Guard great coats proved very useful; in fact I think it was the only coat I had. Most of the journeys were to Aberdeen, but also, now and again, to other east coast ports. On arrival at Aberdeen, regardless of the time of day or night the procedure was much the same, "Awa' an' hae a cup o' tae an' a sleep, loon" (Away and have a cup of tea and a sleep lad), both of which you quickly set about in their bothy.

Two or three hours later you would be wakened, the lorry had been unloaded, washed down, loaded with empty boxes and you were ready for another six to seven hours drive back to Ullapool. What hour of day or night it was made not the slightest difference. The important thing was to get back quickly in the hope of the next load. In the bothy, there were no washing facilities and sleep was on bare wooden benches.

Sometimes, we popped over to the nearby air raid wardens' post. They had warm quarters, more wooden benches and usually a tasty and nourishing boiled kipper. It might be dished up at any point through the night when the wardens had reached the end of another session of their interminable card playing. Space on their wooden benches was sometimes in short supply. I recall one night falling asleep with my head pillowed in an open carton of unwrapped electric light bulbs. When the human body is weary enough, it doesn't much matter.

In Peterhead there was one kippering smokehouse to which I delivered, usually through the night, and the smoker there always chucked a couple of fresh kippers onto an ordinary shovel for me. He placed the shovel on top of his wood chip fire and cooked my 'breakfast' to a turn. Eaten with bare, probably unwashed hands, they were delicious.

Driving with the restricted vehicle lights the wartime blackout regulations permitted was a hazardous business. Meeting oncoming vehicles was tricky. Uncle M was never comfortable about it and hated it. Personally, I deduced that if one aimed at the blackness beside the approaching vehicle lights, that area of road having already been covered by our mutual meagre lighting, should be safe. I never got to putting forward my theory; I was fairly certain it would be rejected.

Driving the *Austin* with its crash gearbox, and lugging at least 20% overload was something of an art. The single-track west highland roads with steep gradients were demanding. Climbing the then formidable hill at Corrie Shalloch required tricky gear shifting right down to first gear – if you missed that one you had a problem. The hand brake was incapable of holding the truck, so from standing hard on the foot pedal you had to achieve a severe hill start – not for the faint hearted.

Engine cooling systems were not very efficient; climbing Corrie Shalloch with anything of a tailwind, the engines on many vehicles reached boiling point. Many little social meetings took place as drivers stopped at the road junction at the top to cool down their roasting engines, sizzling and crackling. Clouds of steam were sent out when the radiator cap was removed for top up of the cooling system from an old wooden tub, itself kept full with a pipe from the adjacent burn. Care had to be exercised when releasing the radiator cap as it could shoot off, propelled by the pressurised steam beneath it.

One time in deep snow in the wood approaching Gairloch, the lower part of my radiator had frozen, but the engine was boiling furiously. As I released the radiator cap, it shot heavenward and disappeared. After a long search, I noticed a small round hole in the snow some twenty feet behind the lorry, and there, at the bottom of it, was the missing cap that had melted its way down to road level.

For the benefit of those who have never experienced a crash gearbox, I'd better explain that the system was normal for the early part of my life, and the now standard refinement of syncromesh was a rarity in Ullapool. To shift gear silently, it was necessary to depress the clutch, select the required gear, adjust the engine revs exactly (using accelerator as necessary) in the new gear to match the revs of the drive shaft (connected to the wheels), and then release clutch at precisely the right moment – to double-declutch as the procedure was called. If you didn't get it right, the gears emitted the most painful noises as one gear fought another for access to mesh. The *Austin* truck was an absolute pig on which to down-shift gears.

It was on an early occasion when Uncle M allowed me to accompany him and do the driving with a load of flour to Garve station, that I qualified in his view to drive unaccompanied. To his silent astonishment (and to mine) I changed from fourth gear to third then to second without even a whisper from the gearbox, a feat I had never heard him achieve. No comment was made, but I had qualified. Later with practice and growing confidence, I learned to do it without even using the clutch; it was really more of a challenge stunt than useful practise. Gear changing with a heavy laden truck on a steep gradient, it was quite possible to literally GRIND to a stand still, in itself a dicey business on a single track road and often with brakes of questionable efficiency – no annual testing then.

On one occasion, I was sent with the *Baby Austin* to take Meg and her first born from Ullapool to her old family home at Opinan (Gairloch), and for some unfathomable reason, the steel rods for operating the brakes had been entirely removed from the 'baby'.

For 'emergency' stops, one soon became expert at rattling down through the gears and finally switching off the engine. At that time, the road from Braemore junction to Aultbea was narrow, single-track gravel surface. Obstacles to its construction, rock projections, etc., had not been removed. Like most highland roads of the time, the road was taken round the obstacles, resulting in hazardous blind bends and corners. The most notorious one was at Gruinard Bay, at the top of the hill known as 'The Cah Baik'. If you were unfortunate enough to meet another vehicle there, you had little option but to reverse some way back down the fierce gradient (reputed to be 1 in 3 at its worst point) and navigate into a passing place – sobering stuff. The thought of it now makes me question our sanity, but that was the way of things and you just got on with it.

During the war, most of the west coast became a 'Protected Area', and for security purposes, had been sealed off, access or exit requiring a military pass. There were road barriers manned by soldiers at Beauly and Laide. Later, the Beauly barrier was moved to Achnasheen.

From time to time, east coast fishermen hired Murdo's lorry for the purpose of taking their nets back to their home base to be changed for others, perhaps of different mesh, size or some other reason. They did this on a Saturday and naturally took the opportunity for a weekend at home. Both ends of the lorry load platform were stacked high with nets, leaving an accommodation space between them. They threw in a few fish boxes for seats, and covered the lot with a tarpaulin. Their well-upholstered behinds didn't seem to mind six hours on a wooden box, moving and constantly rattled by the hard lorry suspension.

On my first such journey, I wondered what the drill would be at the Beauly road barrier. The soldier looked at my pass, said 'OK' and off I went with ten men under the tarpaulin who probably did have passes, but it would have been all the same if they didn't. It was the same on my return, then entering the Protected Area. The hidden passengers seemed to know to stay silent at the appropriate time; on the other hand, perhaps the soldier had no more desire than they had to extend the hold up.

The wartime government soon found it necessary to organise control of all commercial road transport. The west coast hauliers were of independent character and didn't take too well to coming under the jurisdiction of a strong transport firm from the fishing port of Buckie.

The Buckie men had been used to really hard times. Their bosses tended to have near divine authority and their men responded very much cap in hand – 'three bags full, Mr Smith?'

At home, their work entailed a lot of haulage from hard-bitten farmers. The main produce from the farms was oats and masses of barley for the local distilleries. Nowadays, such material is moved in bulk trailers, loaded and emptied untouched by human hand. In 1941 and for long after, it was moved in hessian sacks. The small ones weighed 168lbs (76kgs), while barley came in sacks of 224lbs (101kgs).

At the farms, the full sacks were stored in the upper floor of the farm granary that had a door in the gable end, leading out to a drop of 3-3½ metres. For loading up, the tail end of the lorry was steered and parked just below the granary door and the bags of grain were thrust out onto the shoulders of the unfortunate lorry driver, who then carried and stowed them on his truck. I was still really just a stripling at this time; I could manage the 76kg bags, but the first time a 101kg bag of barley arrived on top of me, my knees simply folded up beneath me.

Working in the 'Buckie concentration camp' as we called it, there was no need for a gymnasium or any other contrived means to develop and strengthen muscles.

The social habits of the majority of male west coasters of the time were such that, at every opportunity – and cash flow permitting – they bolstered themselves with regular intakes of 'the wine of the country' as they often referred to their whisky. Lorry drivers were no exception. Even on a short journey such as Ullapool-Garve, it would be customary to have one or two at *Altguish Inn*. Obviously, as an up and coming, I felt the need to emulate my older companions; gradually, I acquired the resistance to the effects of whisky that most of them had. Thus, they also enjoyed a strong camaraderie. Neither were they strangers to improvisation.

Late one night, I was heading home from Fraserburgh in darkness, closely followed by another truck.

In a remote part of Buchan, the driver started drawing my attention with flashing headlights. I pulled in, to learn that he was just about out of petrol. I was carrying enough for both of us, but neither of us had a container with which to effect a transfer. After a little thought, he suddenly went to his cab and produced a Wellington boot. With the aid of a siphoning tube (an essential bit of gear in those days) and the wellie, we transferred several gallons and all was well.

The *Altguish Inn* of that era had paraffin lamps and a welcoming, open, peat fire. One day when returning to Ullapool, having made my customary social stop, as I was leaving the building, a stranger driver came to me asking for a lift. His words had only just been uttered, when a gunshot rang out. "I'm shot, I'm shot," he yelled. And so he was. The fool, for I can call him nothing else, had a dismantled rifle loaded with a round, wrapped in a great coat under his arm; it had fired and sent a bullet straight through his arm, a hard way to learn.

Following the end of World War II and the establishment of the National Health Service, arrangements were made for every district to have ambulance coverage. Somehow, Uncle M managed to secure the garaging and running of the one for Loch Broom and district. The first one that arrived was an ex-US army left-hand drive *Chevrolet* tin box, which had truck-type running gear and suspension. It was so hard and uncomfortable, that if patients weren't ill before a journey of a minimum 60 miles, they almost certainly would be at its end. It was naturally a 24-hour service and whoever happened to be around when a call came, became ambulance driver – fully <u>un</u>trained. Thankfully, the *Chevrolet* departed and was replaced by an excellent heavy coach-built *Austin* with six cylinder engine and vacuum brakes.

Gradually, the brakes deteriorated till they became totally ineffective. What to do? The Ambulance HQ engineer at

Glasgow had no advice to offer. On a quiet day, unauthorised and mechanically fairly ignorant, I started to explore the braking system and found, underneath the vehicle, a great big vacuum chamber with brake rods going into both ends. I dared to remove it, stuck it on the bench and opened it up. Inside, I found its two operating pistons (one to each rod) totally seized up and unable to move. I freed them off, oiled them, reassembled and installed the unit back where it had come from. Talk about job satisfaction; the brakes were superb. Since then, I've driven many different vehicles of every conceivable size, but I've never found one with brakes to match those of the old *Austin* ambulance.

Since I'm on the subject of ambulances, here's a wee story: It was wintertime with a heavy snowfall, the road to Garve was officially closed to traffic. Uncle M and family were snow-bound at Opinan and I had been left in charge. About six in the evening, the phone rang. It was our local Dr Maclean calling from Badentarbert in Coigach some 25 miles to the north. He had a seriously ill patient and he was bringing him through to Ullapool in his car. He didn't know how long that would take; there was heavy snow lying and it was still snowing. The patient needed to be in hospital at Inverness ASAP. Would I have the ambulance ready and alert the local county council roads department foreman to be available with squad and truck for an escort? High drama!

The foreman told me that he couldn't do that without permission from his HQ at Dingwall. It was after business hours and he couldn't get an answer till next day. Next day, of course, would have been too late as far as the patient was concerned. I pressurised as best I could, but the answer was no, so I told him, "OK, I'll get the poachers to help."

There was a lot of commercial deer poaching going on then – in fact, to the extent that one of the more enterprising of the lads bought a brand new truck to transport his hauls to the Glasgow markets. I'm sure there must have been a lot of heart searching going on in the Roads Department. Those engaged in this new style poaching were not held in high regard locally. My proposed course of action would not look good for the 'Roads'...

I roused one Dan Maclean, alias 'Desperate Dan', from his marital bed of only recent existence. Dan was big, strong and resourceful above all. He gave me the OK and I arranged to pick him up from his dwelling en route on my journey.

It was just short of midnight when Dr Maclean arrived with his patient, the Coigach district nurse and the patient's son, Jim. The patient was transferred and as we made ready for off, I heard a faint and plaintive voice from within – "Is Jim there?" I hastily brought Jim to the ambulance door, and having anticipated some solemn statement, I was somewhat surprised to hear the voice, now a bit stronger, "Have you got my pipe Jim?" The pipe and accompanying tobacco pouch and matches were duly produced and I set off.

Our ambulance by this time had been upgraded to a very plush and comfortable *Humber Super Snipe* model. I picked up Dan and very soon learned other aspects of the *Humber*...

For all its smoothness and power on black roads, it was a miserable performer in deep snow. Our troubles started as we reached heavy drifts on the high ground above Corrie Halloch. The single-track road with its deep drainage ditches was completely blanketed over, with snow merging with the hillsides, or falling ground on one side or the other. The actual location of the road was pure speculation. The ditch might be on either side or even on both.

Passing places on the narrow road had clearly visible signposts. Generally, these were on the same side as the passing place, but sometimes they were on the opposite side. To a large extent, memory played the main part in determining on which side a passing place lay. If you got it wrong, you had big trouble. Mobile phones and two-way radios didn't make their appearance till long afterwards. There would be no other traffic on the road to give help.

The rear end of the *Humber* was fine, but the front end slithered about, to one side or the other at will. Steering had little effect on it.

Progress was mainly in first gear. When the sideways movement became excessive, without pausing the vehicle, Dan got out, put his mighty shoulder against the *Humber*, one side or the other, and squared it up, boarding again when things settled down. Only about a mile past Braemore junction, disaster struck. A slight misjudgement and the ambulance tilted sideways into a deep ditch. I firmly believe there is a higher power that watched over the affairs of my life in this instance…without my giving that a single thought. We were only minutes ditched when we heard the sound of an engine and vehicle lights appeared from where we had come. It was the county road lorry heavily laden with sand, which gave it good traction.

I can only surmise that Dr Maclean had brought about the change of heart. It was only on the way home from Inverness that I learned our patient was suffering from advanced appendicitis, which of course can turn into fatal peritonitis.

The 'rescue' lorry was fit to pull us back onto the road, but he had neither rope nor chain to do it with. Dan and I hurried off to the nearest possible source, the gamekeeper's house at Braemore junction. We quickly roused the gamekeeper from his bed and explained our urgent needs. It was obvious, unusually for the Highlands, that we were not welcome and we drew a blank.

I was keen for him to go to sleep again, because I knew where the solution lay. Running in our direction from his house was an estate fence, and one of the strongest and useful types of wire I've ever come across is old fence wire. In later life, when stuck, I've even used it for welding wire. Having no cutter with us, once we were out of house sight, we got busy and with bare hands worked the wire back and fore till it broke.

After that, it was just a matter of hauling sufficient length for our purpose through the steel up rights. The luxury of work gloves was unheard of. We trailed our loot back to the vehicles, and in quick time, Dan lashed them together with three-fold fence wire, handling it like so much string.

Back on the road I was a bit surprised when I realised the road lorry crew had no intention of coming with us. The journey continued as already described; Dan doing his bit magnificently. Just short of *Altguish Inn*, we met a large four-wheel drive RAF truck with a squad of men and the Chief Constable from Inverness. The RAF tailed us right to Raigmore hospital, at that time just a row of single storey brick buildings.

I later learned that the Chief was brother-in-law to our patient.

From Altguish, the road descends to lower levels and the depth of snow became less, till it became a very slippery, hard-packed surface. The front end of the *Humber* now behaved reasonably, but its tail took up where the front had left off. As I felt it safe to increase speed, it slithered about from side to side, but responded readily to little flicks of the steering wheel.

The chief seemed impressed and later gave a word of congratulation – not good for the ego.

Of course, there was no hospitality at Raigmore, so we headed for home. Full marks to the Coigach nurse and the patient... neither of whom uttered a word of complaint or protest throughout. On the day following, I was somewhat surprised to see our little drama had made the main headline in the *Daily Record* newspaper. I guess news was scarce that day. Best of all, the patient lived for years afterwards; there was a little pat on the back from Dr Maclean as well. One regret I have to this day – Dan, the real hero of the piece didn't get a single mention.

Perhaps I can make amends by recording the following. Like many young men, Dan's earlier days may have been such that he didn't earn his pseudonym for nothing. The story has it that on an occasion, probably in Dingwall, some kind of a fracas arose. Police arrived and a young officer, seeing Dan and having heard something of his reputation, decided it would be best to deal with him first. From behind, he struck him on the head with his baton, whereupon Dan whirled and said to him, "Did you mean that?"

It is not recorded what the response was.

Chapter 5

More about the Period

*A*s the saying goes: 'it takes all kinds…', and the ambulance trips revealed some normally veiled characteristics. There was the old lady who was adamant that the nurse or I had stolen one of her blankets. Even if we had been that way inclined, we really had no need – we were already well equipped. Nevertheless, when we picked her up a second time some months later, as she settled back on her pillows, she lovingly caressed the blanket on her stretcher with the words, "Ah well, my own blanket."

Then it was the same old lady on another day visit to hospital; it was summer time and very hot, and as we left Inverness for home, I pulled in at what was then *Delmore Road House* with the intention of bringing cups of tea out to her and her dear old fellow patient whom she didn't really know. This Mrs Morrison was a native Outer Hebridean, and in spite of her newly broken leg, was probably the most placid person I have ever known. As I approached the open ambulance door bearing my tray of refreshment, I was in time to hear Lady 1 say to Lady 2 in the most exasperated tone, "What I can't understand is how contented you are."

One sunny afternoon I was sent to Little Loch Broom area to pick up an old gentleman and take him to Craig Dunain hospital, Inverness. Craig Dunain was at that time the hospital for patients with psychological problems. Having seen the patient comfortable in the ambulance, I was bending to fold up the rear steps when I heard angry words about a 'greeshan from Ullapool'. At the same time, a stout wooden crutch whistled past my ear. (greeshan – colloquialism – impudent youth).

The general health of Dundonald and district was looked after by a spry old lady, Nurse MacNaughton. When occasion demanded, she was known to ride horseback right round Little Loch Broom and into the Scoraig peninsula, where there was no road. There was little of her, but nothing could daunt her. In later life, she was always recognisable, driving her small car, wearing a trim hat and peering through the steering wheel because she couldn't see over it. My brother-in –law, Sulan, used to call on her with his grocery van. By then, in her eighties, she would often ask him if he would mind reversing her car out of her garage and 'put it pointing to Garve' or Gairloch as occasion might require.

Was it the winter of 42-43? Memory fails me. In any case, the snow and frost was prolonged. Uncle M's lorry was stationed at Gairloch and he with it. In some ways, it suited him, accommodated at his in-laws at Opinan some eight miles from Gairloch pier, and enjoying their relaxed rural way of life so similar to his own early days.

One day, disaster fell. En route to Peterhead, the road ice-bound, somewhere in the Buchan area, he lost it. Truck and road parted company, and he had to leave the truck at Peterhead for repairs to the badly damaged cab. After that I was left to do the truck driving and Uncle M dealt with affairs at home.

* * *

It was a long winter of ice and snow-bound roads. In these conditions, the by now much deteriorated brakes of the *Austin* truck didn't matter much, since to use brakes at all would immediately lock up the wheels and produce an instant tobogganing effect, which in turn, would bring about collision, ditching or worse, depending on the terrain.

Where the Gairloch to Achnasheen road ran for a good eleven miles along Loch Maree side was hazardous at any time. It was a series of single-track, blind twists and turns, apart from some that had been widened for the benefit of naval traffic based at Aultbeh. The majority of the Navy vehicles were fancy *Ford* V8-engined staff cars driven by pretty WRNS (Women's Royal Naval Service) drivers who were mostly no match for the west coast roads.

A gentleman one had to be on the alert for, was a local man with a heavy limp, who had acquired a contract to supply groceries to the Loch Ewe naval base. He transported the goods personally in his own truck. On one occasion, myself stationary, he drove tight against my truck, tearing all my load binding ropes to bits, departed and left me to it. Perhaps the 'wine of the country' played a part!

When the Loch Maree road was ice-bound, it was... Well, it was something else. I was certainly looked after from on high on my journeys. Much later in life, my son Seoras reminded me – "It's good to have friends in high places, Dad."

For my first period of full time driving, I was stationed at Gairloch and for several weeks, the roads, coast-to-coast were ice- and snow-bound. For three solid weeks, I also was snow-bound at Opinan, enjoying the hospitality of the Macaulay household. The only vehicle that seemed to be moving was a local small truck, which most days took a trip over to Gairloch post office and the hotel pub. The rest of the hotel had been commandeered by the Navy for a hospital.

There were no mails to collect at the post office and for a cert, there would be none at the pub, but on a day when I had accompanied the squad on their mission, I found there were other reasons for going there. First, there was quite a delay at the pub and then, about two miles into the return journey, we stopped, and bottles of whisky (home brew), thigh boots and a couple of rifles appeared. There being no glassware available, the deep galvanised lid of a milk pail was utilised to dispense the 'medicine'.

Being keen to sample the home brew, I had a little sip when it was offered – my one and only sample. While it didn't blow my head off, it came near to it. I've been told that when properly matured, the 'brew' was of acceptable quality.

The snow was deep; the mailmen-cum-hunters disappeared up the wooded hillside. I heard no shots fired, and after a lengthy wait, they returned as they went, but ready for a little further refreshment before heading for home.

After three weeks standing, my lorry battery had flattened and unable to start the engine. The solution then was to remove it and carry it probably a mile and a half through the snow to Kenny Long's (real name Mackenzie), the only battery charging facility for miles. Believe me, lorry batteries are not light, I didn't look forward to carrying it back again, but three days later that's what it had to be.

For the next two to three weeks the road conditions remained treacherous.

* * *

My journeys from Gairloch to the east coast ports continued and knowing that the Buckie trucks were sitting safe doing nothing, I finally rebelled. Despatched once more to Gairloch from the east, I was determined to head home to Ullapool instead. It was fully dark by the time I reached Garve.

I looked in to the hotel bar to enquire about the state of the Ullapool road and learned that it was very bad. Nevertheless, I set out on what turned out to be the most nerve-wracking drive I've ever had.

Still the single-track road, the wheel tracks-hard-packed-snow, it was thawed enough to be just wet on top. Wet ice or hard snow are outstandingly the slipperiest surfaces I've ever encountered. I've driven on surfaces where if one left the vehicle, the only way to remain upright was to hold on to its sides.

On this occasion, the track sides were a few inches higher snow than the wheel tracks, and of hard crunchy snow. I hadn't gone far when I found that steering had almost no effect on vehicle direction. The lorry behaved like a locomotive following rails, but with one disturbing difference. It was impossible to know which way the wheels were pointing. Repeatedly, the truck shot off to one side or the other as the steered wheels found a hold and gripped on the hard snow at the side.

On the 'up' gradients I started getting wheel spin. Snow chains existed, but were expensive, thus we didn't have any. I doubt that in the circumstances they would have been much help.

Reluctantly, I stopped and laced my few precious load ropes round my rear wheels. That cured the wheel spin till I started climbing towards Loch Droma. I came to a halt, unable to move back or fore. I climbed out to look at the situation and the wheel ropes had shredded to bits. That would need a bit of explaining at home; any extra expense was not welcomed. Furthermore, I had no right to be there.

Still a teenager, my nerves frayed by the journey to date, I looked around me, then I looked up. All was still – no wind, no sound – all around me, glittering snow and overhead, a countless array of brilliant stars the only light, shining as only they can do in an unpolluted heaven.

What to do? The sight of the starlit heavens had touched me deeply and for the first time in my life, I knelt before God in earnest – in the snow and asked for help.

Almost immediately, the answer came. I rose, reached into the cab for my Home Guard great coat and stuffed it in front of the rear wheels on one side. But grip would be needed on both sides and I had nothing else...or so I thought...

Suddenly another answer; I peeled of my jacket and stuck it in front of the other wheel.

Making the gentlest start I could, I rolled into motion. It was a good two hundred yards before I came to a place of neutral gradient and stopped, the truck perched on a slight crown of road. Stopping anywhere else, I knew I wouldn't be able to get away again. I hurried back down the road, collected coat and jacket apparently none the worse of their abuse.

In hindsight, I realise I didn't even have the good grace to say thanks to God.

Climbing towards Loch Droma again, the wet road had frozen, giving better grip and once over the top, it was a downhill doddle.

There was no such luxury as a watch or dashboard clock. Rolling into Ullapool, I was surprised to see the *Caley* bar still lit up. Inside, I found Uncle M and cronies happily socialising and to my pleasant surprise I, received a warm welcome.

Occasionally at Gairloch, circumstances required my spending a night at the pier area. There was a very convenient driver accommodation quite near the pier, in a low-roofed corrugated iron bungalow known as '*The Tea Rooms*'.

There were no niceties about personal tastes. Where there was space available in a double bed, that's where one slept, along with whoever had already laid claim to the other half.

The Tea Rooms proprietor incidentally was a devout Free Presbyterian and, I trust also, Christian. There were odd occasions when drivers had to depart on a Sunday morning, and no matter how much was owed, that gentleman would no way accept payment. He simply said he would get it next time.

Loch Droma, near Ullapool

There was a night during the snow period when I didn't get much sleep. My bed companion turned out to be a fish buyer of unpleasant character whose advances had to be forcibly repelled during the night. An hour or two later, he apparently lost his reason totally; I had to rouse the household and an ambulance and medics quickly turned up from the naval hospital at the hotel, to remove him. Thankfully I never saw him again.

Apart from sleeping in the cab which drivers often had to do, I think the Gairloch bungalow was the coldest sleep I used to have. When sleep got the upper hand on the road, you simply stopped the engine and immediately fell asleep just sitting in the driver's seat. There wasn't room for anything else. Usually after an hour or so, you awakened, shivering with cold and aching with cramps. Once under way, the renewed engine heat gradually restored circulation.

* * *

I cannot go on without reference to our Buckie Transport boss at Ullapool. I'll call him Alex; he was of immense strength. Other Buckie men used to tell that before the war came along and elevated him to being a local manager, Alex used to take his own lorry out to a farm, and single-handed, load it with 2-cwt sacks of barley, and complete his first delivery before anyone else had started in the morning.

One day, while he was having a quite drink in Ullapool's *Caley Bar*, an ill-advised stranger tried to pick a quarrel with him and threatened to strike him. Alex quietly told him that if he did, it would be the worst thing he ever did in his life. The adversary thought better of it and backed off – a wise move.

Sometimes on a Saturday, and Alex needed transport home for the weekend, it seemed to 'happen' that there would be a small load left over for Buckie. I would fall heir to it – and to Alex – as passenger. On the first such trip, while bowling along at 30 – 40mph, he suddenly opened his door, rose from his seat and was making for outdoors, as I, being unfamiliar with his method of handling the calls of nature, tried vainly to make an emergency stop. I immediately received the following instruction, "Dinna stop, loon, haud her gauin, a'm jist gonnae hae a pumpship."

It surely takes all kinds.

Since I'm on the subject of attending to calls of nature – there was an occasion during the war period when I was sent with Uncle M's saloon to Garve railway station, there, to collect from an arriving train, Lady X and her entourage who were coming to Ullapool for a holiday. Adjacent to the 'south arrivals' platform, the stationmaster had set up in the station yard, a hen-house and wire mesh hen-run to help with kitchen supplies. I had loaded the luggage and all, except Lady X who seemed to have disappeared. Visually casting about, imagine my surprise when I beheld her inside the hen-run, squatting with skirt hoisted, attending to the natural call.

The irony of the situation was not lessened by the fact that not long after, I read a press article on the publication of her book on ETIQUETTE!

* * *

Then there was the story of Rorie whose house was high on a steep hillside. At certain times, tups (male sheep) can become fairly aggressive. Their method of diffusing their aggression is to charge their opponent and butt severely with their bone hard heads. On the occasion in question, having somewhat over-indulged, Rorie, making his way uphill on all fours, was challenged by a stout tup. A passer-by overheard his response, "Come on then, I'll teach you some science."

The outcome of the event was not recorded.

* * *

Our Ullapool mail bus was not as young as it once was. New vehicles were pretty well unobtainable in the war years. John, its driver, was also getting on, and he didn't suffer fools gladly. One day at Garve station, he was thrusting the Ullapool mail bags into their compartment when a newly arrived old dear from the far south approached and with her mouth full of marbles enquired from him if this was the bus for Ullapool. We were not into destination boards and such like. Upon John's affirmative reply, she foolishly said, "Oh, what a quaint old thing!"

I think she would have been unprepared for John's reply (he tended to be slow and positive in his speech), "Yes, and there's some quaint old things go in it."

Chapter 6

The RAF

*T*he war had not long finished, when to my surprise, I received a buff coloured OHMS (On His Majesty's Service) envelope. Inside were a rail warrant, giving free travel, and instructions to report some days later to RAF Padgate in Lancashire. Although I had volunteered long before, to my disappointment I had now become a conscript.

A long time earlier, Uncle M had, I think with tongue in cheek, passed on to me a rebuke from the head man in Buckie about some misdemeanour I was accused of. Mr Buckie said that I should be grateful to him, as he had been instrumental in keeping me out of the *Sodgers*, as he called the military, to which Uncle M had responded, "I don't suppose he would thank you for that."

In hindsight, Mr Buckie probably had more wisdom than I had.

Wartime austerity was still very much the order of the day. All the 'necessities' of life were strictly rationed; for example, two ounces of butter per person per week. Strangely, one exception was bread, which was still freely available. Bread brings me to another short tale.

After some months in the RAF, I had completed a course of instruction on electrical work as applied to aircraft, vehicles and marine craft as they chose to call boats.

My lot were paraded on the square, prior to our first major home leave. The rationing of bread had not long been instigated in the nation. A crisp little Warrant Officer (a formidable rank to us novices) had taken over the parade and issued sharp, concise, verbal instructions on our way ahead, finishing with the standard "ANY QUESTIONS?" – the latter in tones that strongly suggested it would be best not to have any.

A timid and cultivated voice spoke from the back of the ranks, "What shall we do about bread sir?"

Now, in those days, the services however tough they might be in other ways, were not given to coarse language in communicating with lower ranks. Nevertheless, our Warrant Officer succumbed to temptation and quick as a flash, his response to the question came clear and crisp, "Use your ------- loaf, PARA...A...ADE... DIS...MISS."

* * *

Padgate, I think, is somewhere in the Preston area in Lancashire. I left Ullapool for RAF Padgate on our local mail bus on a grey January morning. To my surprise, I had a travelling companion – David Macrae, son of an Ullapool publican. He was headed for the same destination. I thought he was of a somewhat gloomy disposition, and after arrival at Padgate, we had little contact.

Even in January, steam train travel can be quite comfortable, with steam heating through the carriages. In our case, we had the necessary installation, but not the steam – result...considerable discomfort.

I don't recall having a meal on the journey; just a wee pack of sandwiches from home. About six a.m. the following morning, a motley crew of shivery young men converged on the main entrance to RAF Padgate, as no doubt thousands had done before. It was still dark, with freezing fog. Facing us was a silent, armed sentry. After some hesitation, a voice from somewhere said, "Can we come in?"

With obvious satisfaction, the sentry responded, "Yes, mate, your problem will be getting out."

How right he was!

Wooden hut billets were quickly allocated and like homing pigeons, we located the cookhouse. The whole place was grubby and shouting out for demolition. The toilet facilities were the pits – no lighting, window glass all smashed, freezing cold water and a mini-gale blowing through. Shaving thus in the darkness with old style razors was torture.

* * *

Shut in like prisoners, we welcomed a couple of days later the next move – by train to RAF Kimbolton in Bedfordshire.

* * *

Our first day on the station was spent taking the dining hall trestle tables outdoors, turning them over and scraping masses of discarded Yankee chewing gum from their undersides.

For a further eight weeks, we didn't see outside the perimeter wire; our new station quickly became known as Kimbelsen. It turned out to have been an American air force base, with fancy American Nissen huts that leaked like sieves; their one redeeming feature was their paraffin burning heating stoves. Their fronts were beautifully chrome plated; they stood in the middle of the floor, one to a hut and they had fat metal chimneys rising and going out through the roof.

It didn't take long to observe that their paraffin feed was regulated by a carburettor-like device. By tying down its float, we found that the paraffin flow and heat output were wonderfully increased. After an hour or so, the chimney could be made to glow red almost to the roof. It was a great asset in the freezing nights of January.

Things were not improved by the heating system for our toilet block, being frequently out of action. It was a hard winter, but it toughened us up. Wherever we looked on this vast, exposed air-field, it appeared impossible to see its boundaries – just endless expanses of runway, straddling miles of hoar frosted grass. There, from dawn till dusk, we drilled, ran and sweated, while our instructors bawled their heads off, keeping us informed of what an inept lot we were.

But, by the end of the standard eight weeks, we could have given a good account of ourselves against a regiment of guards.

A curiosity of the system was a German corporal drill instructor, who introduced himself by nationality and the announcement that, "I'm a bastard...a German bastard," then did his utmost to confirm the matter by every conceivable means. He had been in the UK at the outbreak of war and had been interned in the Isle of Man as an enemy alien. He was released into the RAF Regiment, who supplied all drill instructors.

So easily I also might have been in the Isle of Man. Born in Chile and my birth registered with the British consul in Magallanes, I was classed a 'dual national', i.e. Chilean/British till I became of military age.

In WW2, Chile was not looked on with favour by the 'Allies'. It was seen, although theoretically neutral, as a country kindly disposed to Germany and its naval vessels. Thus, just prior to my 18th birthday, I received a Home Office letter spelling out my position and requiring me to choose a single nationality. One way or the other, I would be in the British forces, or interned (along with my German corporal) in the Isle of Man.

Yet one more incident from Kimbelsen comes to mind – when we had been allocated Corporal Wildgoose for our training in the use of bayonets.

Uttering fearsome yells, we did the usual thing – severely wounding suspended bags of straw. For the final turn, he set us up on some higher ground and required us, on command, to charge down with fixed bayonets towards the crate that was his chosen stance for the occasion.

Somehow, I happened to be a bit ahead of the rest. The sight and sound of me charging towards him with fixed bayonet and yelling unintelligible Gaelic battle cries was too much for *Wild Duck*, as we preferred to call him, and he turned and ran.

* * *

At the end of our eight weeks, for the first time since joining the RAF, we were released into the outside world, and the Scots amongst us had for most, our first experience of an English pub. It was emphasised to us that we were representing the RAF and had better behave accordingly. It was considered that up to that time there was a danger that our bearing, etc. might disgrace the uniform. In the local, I was introduced to the game of darts. On my second or third throw, I managed to skewer the cable to the light over the dart board bringing the game to an immediate end, and the landlord, I'm sure, was glad to see the back of us.

Next day, three others and I were issued with pack lunches, rail warrants and instructions to report to RAF Calshot. Having muddled our way there, Calshot turned out to be a 'winding down' flying boat base on Southampton Water.

Directed down its long spit of land, we encountered a Warrant Officer, whom we greeted with smart salutes and stated our case. His reaction was, "Cut out all that stuff. This is RAF Calshot, we don't go in for that here."

Our presence appeared to be something of an embarrassment. Within days, we were on the move again, this time to RAF Mountbatten at Plymouth.

Mountbatten was a kind of Shangri-la; modern accommodation with central heating, on a narrow neck of land projecting into Plymouth Sound. Spring had sprung and most of the personnel were redundant war service people awaiting their discharge.

Discipline accordingly was very relaxed. Duties were minimal and the old hands regaled us with air sea adventures from the 'Med'.

Plymouth had been a base for flying boats and HSLs (high speed rescue launches), the remnant of which were now riding at anchor.

A 'Med' tale, told me by a Sergeant, concerned an enemy air attack while rescuing a downed pilot. The launch commander one Snaky ------ had jumped overboard. Under threat of a Sten gun, he was ordered back aboard by one of his own crewmen. I mention him because he's going to turn up again.

* * *

Plymouth itself was full of interest. Our transport to town was by a ferry that landed us at the Mayflower steps, from where the founding fathers of the USA, the Pilgrim Fathers had set sail so long ago. Then, there was Plymouth Hoe of Drake fame, and the town centre shops were all Nissen huts, the originals having been blown to bits in German air raids. Idyllic days, glorious weather, near to no responsibilities, well clothed, sheltered and fed, came to an end with new postings to a large 'trades training' establishment in Wiltshire.

With kit bags, rail warrants and stony broke, on a glorious summer day, four of us set out from Plymouth station for Melksham camp. The connection between smoking and cancer had not yet been established and we were all cigarette smokers – when we could afford them.

On that particular day, we possessed one cigarette between us and we carefully shared draws on the way to Bristol where we were to change trains. As there was more than an hour to wait for the next train, we laid our kitbags on the station platform in front of a row of slot machines. Three of us had already sat down on the kitbags to bask in the sunshine.

While we were ruing the want of a cigarette to complete our bliss, our fourth member arrived saying, "Never mind, lads, providence will provide," whereupon he slumped down on his kitbag, thumping heavily against the slot machine behind.

Immediately, the machine emitted a few clicks and a louder one as its drawer popped open revealing a pristine, cellophane wrapped packet of twenty cigarettes.

"What did I tell you?" said wee Alex as he triumphantly reached up for them.

In recounting the incident, I don't wish to imply that the provision had been activated by the Almighty. It was none the less enjoyed by the recipients.

* * *

Melksham turned out to be a pleasant town, home of the Avon tyre factory. The camp, about a mile and a bit out of town, had row upon row of wooden billet huts with some 10,000 residents on various courses.

I was thankful I was in the RAF, as I witnessed a Fleet Air Arm trainee on punishment being doubled round the parade ground for

81

a long period, holding a heavy rifle over his head. Every time his pace slackened in the slightest or the rifle wavered even a trifle, his attendant Petty Officer instantly bellowed him back to maximum performance.

I found the RAF's three months electrical course intense and fascinating. There were a few redundant aircrew on the course, retraining for a permanent ground role. As they gradually learned the potential hazards of the aircraft systems of the time, more than one vowed he would never fly again.

The last week of our training was spent resolving a multitude of amazing faults on a full mock up of the wiring of a four-engine bomber. There were crossed wires and all sorts every which way – absolutely nothing worked. Most of us made it with a day in hand.

Our last day was spent restoring chaos to the circuits for those coming after us.

There followed a fortnight's home leave after which we were dispersed to various postings. For me, it turned out to be RAF Corsewall, flying boat and air sea rescue base on the south shore of Loch Ryan, and a few miles out of Stranraer. By that time the flying boats had all been hauled ashore, but the fast launches were still in the water. RAF Corsewall was also home to a contingent of German POWs (prisoners of war), one of whom was allocated to our electrical (Nissen hut) department. I had an instant soft spot for Helmut from Hamburg, who in his yellow-patched prisoner garb tended to look pretty miserable. Each day as the NAAFI van came round with tasty bites for our elevenses, I always bought for Helmut as well.

The technical skills of the Germans were way beyond ours; we seemed like boy scouts in comparison. They did a nice sideline for themselves producing and selling pretty, domestic items, fashioned from the perspex port holes of the stranded flying boats. I recall fluted edge fruit bowls, finished with hand painted decorations. They also made smart looking table cigarette boxes.

There came a day when I was required to install a freshly

charged battery in the confined bow space of a small marine tender. I was still green to the hazard of hydrogen gas in a newly charged battery.

Having wrestled the heavy battery into position, I was crouched on all fours over it, and scarcely room to move. It was a day of strong wind and the boat was restless in the water as I was making my final connection. A slight slip of my spanner, a flash of electricity and there was an almighty bang. By a miracle, no acid reached my face or hands, but disaster, disaster, the whole end was blown clean out of the battery case.

As my companion and I contemplated the situation, and the prospect of retribution to come, suddenly Helmut came to the rescue. With gestures and his minimal English, he took over, saying, "My freent (friend) OK."

By next morning, the battery was back, not quite as good as new, but with its casing complete and in working order.

* * *

In Corsewall, the Germans were organised. They seemed to have a man in every department; things were scarce, but any item we had difficulty obtaining, they usually produced at a day's notice. Helmut had served on the Russian front in the dreadful winter of '42. He described how the Russian airborne troops had jumped from their low flying slow aircraft straight into heavy snowdrifts without parachutes, probably with guns at their backs.

* * *

The Loch Ryan weather became wintry, and once more with American hutting and their excellent paraffin stoves, at least our evenings were warm. The technical servicing facilities stood on the inland side of the main road running along the south side of Loch Ryan. The now almost defunct flying boat section was located just along the road from us. Its C.O. (Commanding Officer) had somehow managed to hang on to a 'Walrus' amphibian aircraft, which he apparently kept simply for his own amusement.

I should think that by now, only enthusiasts would have any idea what a *Walrus* looked like. A *Walrus*, even by the standards of those days, was the most primitive looking biplane amphibian aircraft. Its wings appeared to be mounted immediately above the fuselage, and its large radial engine was installed between them, its airscrew, or propeller, pointing rearwards. Thus, instead of pulling the aircraft along, it rather pushed it and was referred to as a 'pusher'.

Others and I were greatly intrigued when we first witnessed Mr. C.O. going for one of his jaunts. Alerted by the roar of the *Walrus* engine, our eyes swung towards it and, with fascination, watched it roll out the very wide gate on its own wheels, and engine roaring, it crossed the main road onto the concrete slipway leading down into the loch. Once afloat, no doubt with wheels retracted, it cruised out to start its lengthy takeoff run and staggered into the air – in due course returning in reverse order.

* * *

As the winter petered out, suddenly marching orders again – this time to RAF Felixstowe, straight into spring in Suffolk and excellent permanently built quarters almost on the North Sea water front. There was even a white tiled bathroom, complete with reliable hot water supply. Pretty soon, a new Catering Warrant Officer came on the scene. He was obviously accustomed to professional chef standards and the usually mediocre food suddenly became top class, as he personally supervised everything that went on.

There were still several *Sunderland* flying boats moored on buoys offshore. Out our main gate and across an expanse of railway sidings, there was a small dock with narrow entrance, thus forming a safe harbour for a small still active fleet of high speed rescue launches, slower pinnaces, seaplane tenders and small fast open launches. The dock also supported the transport needs of a large flour mill standing on its edge and still bringing in its wheat by that most picturesque of sailing vessels, ancient Thames barges – wheat in, flour out.

Also at the dock was the engineers and electricians base, a Nissen hut with work benches and the standard cylindrical solid fuel stove, and in charge of all, amiable 'Chiefy' (Flight Sergeant) Bill Boyce, patiently waiting the day of his discharge. Bill had joined the 'airworks' when it was still the Royal Flying Corps.

The electricians having nearly nothing to do, I soon teamed up with a delightful little Lancastrian, Corporal Fitter Bob Wilding, who mainly serviced and generally cared for most of the marine engines. Most of these were *Perkins Diesels*, a complete novelty to me, being familiar only with petrol engines and their spark plugs, etc. These noisy *Perkins* had neither spark plugs nor much else recognisable to me. Bob Wilding, an old hand, soon tutored me in every aspect of them, knowledge which has stood me in good stead for most of my working life.

Most interesting of all for me were the rescue launches, powered by three *Napier* 500 bhp ex-aero engines, which had been hastily converted for marine use, and from air cooling to water cooling. When these were 'wound up' and run even at moderate speeds, the noise in the tiny engine room was shattering. I was fascinated with the starting procedure. While one man was pressing the starter button, a second applied a couple of 'ping-pong' style bats to the flat air intakes to act as a choke on two of each engine's three carburettors. Two banks of cylinders banged and burst into life, sometimes backfiring with stabs of flame shooting from the air intakes, and a bat was hastily applied to bank number three. As it picked up, further speech became impossible.

My apologies for the foregoing to non-technical readers.

* * *

Hector, RAF 1946

The winter of 1946-47 was memorable – for six weeks continuous hard frost and heavy snowfalls nation wide, trains stranded in snowdrifts and many other difficulties. I have recently read that that winter seals were seen on ice-flows in the Beauly Firth. For the first time in my life I saw the sea frozen. Nothing could move in our dock and the ice extended out beyond the moored flying boats. I experienced my hands sticking to the steel rungs of the pier ladders. The NAAFI van with our elevenses was eagerly welcomed, and as we partook in the open, one or two slow drinkers found their tea froze solid in their mugs.

* * *

Winter passed, came spring and a glorious summer. Life in Felixstowe was pleasant. The activities of an RAF experimental unit provided interest as they tested out their various productions.

86

These included large ten man rubber dinghies, covered in, as opposed to the smaller wartime ones in which the occupants were fully exposed to the elements.

Our base housed a training school for motorboat crewmen. From their complement, the crafty experimental types used to recruit eager volunteers for their dinghy tests. The procedure was simple, a brief word of instruction, aircrew type one-piece suits, a life jacket (survival suits had not yet made their appearance), a trip out into the North Sea, and the unfortunates were cast adrift in the latest dinghy.

Next morning, they would be located and 'rescued', most of them having been violently sick. Nobody ever volunteered a second time.

Probably the most astonishing experimental production concerned the previously mentioned *Walrus* type amphibian.

On a bright summer day, a couple of us saw one taxiing on the Orwell estuary when suddenly there was a blast of thick black from behind it and it shot into the sky with a heavy black smoke trail – as someone once said, like a homesick angel. I don't think there were any more rocket assisted Walrus take-offs.

* * *

In those days, service discipline required that 'Other Ranks' on meeting an officer anywhere, acknowledged the fact with a smart salute. There was a day when Paddy Murphy, in town when he shouldn't be, inadvertently encountered the Station Adjutant, and keeping a low profile, totally ignored him. Paddy was quickly taken to task, and received no mean dressing down. By one of the odd twists of life, the scene was repeated on the same afternoon, and Mr. Adjutant was some angry. When he eventually had had his say, Paddy responded with the following, "Well, Sor (sir), on account of the few words we had in the morning, I didn't think you and I were speaking now."

What followed is not recorded.

* * *

One day, I was suddenly ordered to pack my bags and take myself to RAF Lyme Regis in Dorset. Lyme Regis was then a delightful English small town with an old stone harbour, and home to a small marine craft unit, total complement twenty-five personnel. The launches were used for target towing for aircraft in The Channel. My duties were near to zero. I looked after a small battery charging room, which never had any batteries and once about every three weeks, I was Duty Man for the day. Duty consisted of hoisting the station flag each morning and lowering it at evening. In the services this procedure is normally accompanied with lots of military ceremony, but not in Lyme Regis. Unusually, personnel dressed more or less as they felt inclined. The Duty Man would pocket the flag, open the street door and peer both ways. If no one was around, he then nipped across the street to where the flagpole stood and did what he had to do. Around eight in the evening the procedure was reversed and everyone was happy.

I said earlier that Snaky ----- would turn up again...and sure enough, he did. At Lyme Regis he was the Officer Commanding the station. He ran a profitable little sideline in the form of a barrel of beer. On the hot summer days, one could slake one's thirst for little expense from Snaky's barrel. To add to his pleasures, he had a beautiful live-in Danish blonde.

The local hostelries, in addition to beer and spirits, also sold rough cider or 'scrumpy' as it was known. Scrumpy cost six old pence per pint, equating to 2½ pence in current coinage. Since my earnings amounted to £2.22 per fortnight by present standards, if strong drink was to be partaken of, the general leaning was to scrumpy – and strong it certainly was. Two pints was sufficient to render most people distinctly drunk.

One morning, we awoke to find a penny in the 'slot' weighing machine in our billet. It was a fine looking machine of the type commonly seen outside chemists' shops of the period. Apparently, Ginger, one of our cooks, having overdone it with the scrumpy had taken a fancy to it on his way home and had brought it with him. Fortunately, it could be returned to its rightful location without fuss.

On a glorious summer day, probably out of pure boredom, I was lying under a truck studying its underside in our garage-cum-boathouse, when suddenly two pairs of trouser-clad legs came to a halt beside my projecting feet. The owner of the 'civvy' trousers was plying our Snaky with questions suitable for the occasion while I lay 'doggo'. I'm sure Snaky must have wondered what on earth I was doing, but no questions were asked then or afterwards. I later discovered that our visitor was no less a personage than the Under Secretary of State for Air, who I suspect was out for a pleasant day at the Lyme Regis seaside.

* * *

With a couple of days notice, I was suddenly moved back to Felixstowe. Whilst changing railway stations in London via the Underground, I was lugging my kitbag up a steep stairway when I noticed a colleague from my old barrack room at Felixstowe, descending and similarly encumbered. We stopped for surprised greetings and a short blether, and he pulled from his inner pocket, a postal letter ex-Felixstowe, which he had been intending to give to me. Where was he headed? Lyme Regis! It's a funny old world.

A little known fact of Lyme Regis is that it was the landing site chosen by William of Orange, when he arrived to become King of England in what was known as the Monmouth rebellion.

Among the interesting characters at Felixstowe, was a pleasant Jamaican engine fitter known to all as Sikh. I don't think any of us knew any other name for him. He was handsome, with woolly Afro'-Caribbean hair that he laboriously and meticulously trimmed himself, using a handheld second mirror for the back. RAF regulation-wise he appeared to be a law unto himself, ignoring dress regulations, etc. He often went up to London at weekends. On one such occasion, he ordered three tailor-made suits for his leisure wear, while most of us were into swapping scarce civvy jackets, etc. for off-duty times.

On another occasion, Sikh was locked up in the guardroom for a period. I don't remember why, but most likely he would have been AWOL for a few days. Felixstowe guardroom, single storey with a flat roof, was built in classic prison style surrounding an open-air exercise area. The windows looking onto the exercise yard had long steel spikes projecting inwards from above them. When Sikh was being given his daily airing, the duty RAF policeman always had a nasty-tempered Alsatian dog held on a chain. As Sikh walked round and round, each time he came near the dog, he tormented and provoked it. Finally, the dog's tolerance gave out and it broke free. Quick as a flash, Sikh jumped, grabbed a window spike and swung himself onto the flat roof. For all his customary nonchalant gait, there was still a bit of jungle agility in him.

Another pleasant personality was Blackie, ex-trawler man from Fleetwood. Although called Blackie, he had wavy light auburn hair. He obviously had no intention of knuckling down to the RAF regime and fought it all the way, resulting in several lengthy periods in the main military prison at Colchester. He was an expert boatman whom I am sure would have been much better employed back on his trawler. He told me he had done several periods of 'solitary' in Colchester in total darkness. He said the most treasured item to smuggle into solitary was a pin. Sanity was maintained by throwing it at random and then spending the time searching for it. 'They' never broke Blackie and he maintained his campaign of rebellion to the end.

There came a day when little Paddy Docherty bolted from his escorting RAF policeman and disappeared from the scene. By and large, Paddy spent more of his life locked up in the guardroom than he did out of it. The RAF police did their utmost to find him. Eventually, a week later, he was flushed out from a captured

German flying boat, which lay on our station. We never saw Paddy again and I'm sure Colchester received one more resident.

Post War social life was getting off the ground again in Felixstowe; life was pleasant enough – the weather with East Anglian sunshine, and odd trips to sea in the motor launches.

Sergeant Chisholm from Inverness was redundant aircrew and an amateur radio 'ham' (enthusiast). One pleasant summer evening he suddenly picked up on his personally built radio, a 'MAYDAY' call from an aircraft down – in the sea – off Ostend. Quickly, word was passed and a rescue launch scrambled. Shorty Fauschan was the duty coxswain. The days for a standby launch were well past and Shorty, without charts for the continental coast and possibly having forgotten some of his navigational skills, a bit panicky, urgently enquired where Ostend lay. The response was 'first right past the Cork lightship'. He set sail, but the situation died a natural death without any published conclusion.

* * *

New Year rolled round and on the 17th April 1948, my desired notice of 'demob' came along. Full of curiosity and anticipation about my future, with others I journeyed by train to No 101 RAF Personnel Dispersal Centre, Kirkham, at Bircham Newton, I think in Lancashire. There I was to hand in all my RAF things, including the tiny 'housewife' needle and thread case that had been standard issue. I came out the other end in a full set of civilian clothes, complete with a smart blue suit, which served me as 'best' for years after, and the cherry on the cake, a month's pay from the RAF.

Chapter 7

£5 a Week

I wasn't long home till Uncle Murdo said I could join his other employee, Angie – this time on pay, £5 a week .The duties were those generally associated with a small country style garage and vehicle hiring business. About the same time, I received an offer to work with the local power station staff of the North of Scotland Hydro-Electric Board. In the event, I decided to stay with the family, although in hindsight, I don't think I really felt part of it.

I soon discovered that payment for overtime work was not favoured by Ullapool employers, although I was virtually on call at all times, and not unusually would work right round the clock when necessary. I did have the bonus of a roof over my head, meals and my laundry done for me. I think that at the end of the day, it gave me a good sense of values. My day normally started with a school run before breakfast, taking children to Ullapool mainly from Strath Kanaird, and for periods from further away, Drumrunie and Achnamerchan. The roads involved were single track, gravel surfaced with abundance of 'pot' holes, which in the mainly wet weather were full of water, while at other times the entire road sent up clouds of dust.

For a long time, the school run vehicle was an ex-Government wartime ambulance, a 1928 *Austin '20'* conversion from a saloon body. Thus, by the time I met it, it was a full twenty years old. Uncle M had again converted its interior to two long bench seats and a square cut back, closed to half its height and with two small hinged doors secured by external slip bolts. The upper half was wide open to whatever was coming, showers of spray, or clouds of dust. With these, the unfortunate children were generously anointed.

The pulling power of the *Austin* was such that at one particularly steep section of road, one had to come down to a very slow
second gear. Gauge my surprise when one sunny day, sensing a
movement to my right, I beheld one of my livelier passengers
some yards away, overtaking the *Austin* on the heather hillside.
He remounted without difficulty. I recently met him at an
Ullapool funeral; he was now a grey haired and moustached,
comfortable-looking Inverness lawyer.

Forgive me if I continue a little about the *Austin*. Changing up,
the gearbox had a long delay between gears as the heavy fly-
wheeled engine lazily lost sufficient revs to allow engagement of
the next gear. Thus it was necessary to remain in a low gear till
any gradient had relaxed to near level. Changing down, one had to
get everything just right, or you very soon ground to a halt.

In my post-RAF enthusiasm, I decided to apply a grease gun as
appropriate to the *Austin*'s heavy steering mechanism. Well
pleased with my work, I was somewhat taken aback when Uncle
M, having done a school run himself, took me to task in stern
tones. Had I greased the *Austin*? On my 'yes' response, he issued
the following rebuke, "Well, never do that again, I could hardly
keep it on the road."

The *Austin*'s demise eventually arrived when the children's
parents rebelled and complained to the education authority.

Its successors were in turn two old *Chrysler* seven-seaters. These
American petrol guzzlers – each had but three forward gears. They
struggled hard when on my runs with hefty fishing crews to the east
coast ports. Their braking tended to be less than adequate, clearly
more suited to the wide-open spaces of America than our meagre
Highland road systems. Like the *Austin* before them, they served
for a time and went their way. One day, I commented to Uncle M
on the high petrol consumption of one of them. "Oh, it's not bad,"
he said, "it does at least thirteen miles to the gallon."

My colleague Angie (Baldy) was a most pleasant person to work
with. He himself was not blessed with a great crop of hair, but the

'Baldy' identification originally applied to his father, a hardy old man of the sea. Thus, as Ullapool had several Angies, this particular one was identified by the extra tag of 'Baldy'. Angie's mother, too, had been a pleasant old lady, who in her day had known her share of hardship. In WW2, Angie like many of his contemporaries, had been with the Seaforth Highlanders and in 1940, was taken prisoner by the Germans in their push into France.

There followed five long years as a prisoner of war. Meanwhile, his faithful spaniel Rover lived long enough to see him home again, I'm sure with great joy.

I continue about Angie because he was a unique and most resourceful man.

The terminals of spark plugs in motorcar engines at that time were fully exposed; they had no insulation although they carried some 10,000 volts. From time to time, a plug would foul up and cease to function. The common practice to identify the offending plug was to, in turn, connect each plug terminal to the engine metal work with a wooden handled screw driver, thus rendering the plug temporarily ineffective – all this with the engine running. The one that made no difference to the engine note was of course the plug that had to be cleaned or changed.

If a careless finger or hand accidentally touched a terminal, the human body received a fairly strong electric shock to which very few people were willing to subject themselves. Angie, however, was quite impervious to such shocks. Despising the use of a screwdriver, he would take hold of each terminal in turn to make his diagnoses.

One day, a well-heeled looking gent arrived at our garage with a *Daimler* car. *Daimlers* were rather up-market, and unusual to be seen in Ullapool. Despite its expensive nature, the *Daimler* had a faulty plug. As Angie raised its bonnet to investigate, its owner leaned with his elbow on the front corner, that he might better observe what was happening. Just before he took hold of the first spark terminal, Angie politely asked him to take his elbow off the car. This he did, but in no time resumed his former stance, only to receive a rude 10,000-volt awakening. Before he could say anything, Angie reminded him that he had told him to take his elbow off the car. Despite some ruffled feathers, he and his *Daimler* departed, with his problem solved.

One of Angie's great gifts was that he never lost his cool. One day on a blind bend on the narrow gravel road north from Ullapool, he very suddenly met an ill-prepared tourist with an expensive car. The man lost control and drove his car into the ditch, his female passengers being no doubt shaken in the process. Both drivers came out of their vehicles, and the holidaymaker also lost control of his temper. He proceeded to berate Angie with all kinds of threats, including reporting the matter to the police. Turning towards the car, he asked his wife to hand out his notebook and pen. The notebook came OK, but unfortunately she couldn't find the pen. With a little smile, Angie reached into his pocket and proffered a pen. The pen was refused, the notebook slammed shut and Angie took his leave promising to summon help.

On account of some alleged misdemeanour, one lovely summer's evening Uncle M, who tended to be 'short-fused', lay in wait for Angie as he returned from a lorry trip.

In the middle of the street, he angrily addressed Angie at some length. As he ran out of steam, Angie, unruffled, quietly won the round with the words, "Well, goodnight, I'll see you in the morning."

* * *

Since I have earlier mentioned Achnamerchan, and almost nobody will have heard of it, solitary and remote a couple of miles into the hills north of Strath Kanaird, it consisted of one shepherd's house where he and his young family lived. Having bought a small car, he had someone drive it into a nearby, level field for him, and there he taught himself to drive. Even had he wanted a school of motoring, in the north-west Highlands, no such thing had been heard of at that time.

I recall being told of an old farmer in the Black Isle, who having got hold of his first tractor, was seen going round and round a big field, vainly trying to bring the thing to a halt, and shouting, "Whoa, you butch."

I suppose inevitably 'in spring a young man turns to thoughts of love' and I was no exception. I guess it is not much different for the opposite gender, and happily my thoughts appeared to be reciprocated by lovely Rebecca Ross. She was not only lovely in appearance, but also in character and nature. She had beautiful natural wavy hair that required nothing more than a tidy up with a comb to give the appearance of having newly emerged from a high-class hairdresser – the envy of her female friends and acquaintances.

* * *

She didn't have an easy early life. Her mother was widowed on the same night that Rebecca's younger brother, Willie, was born. There was no widow's pension or child allowance; Maggie Ross did a quick training in hairdressing in Greenock, staying with her sister Liza who was married there. Returning to Ullapool, she set up in business and lived in tiny premises beside the pier. Her in-laws, old Seoras Ross and his wife were helpful to her. In old age, both of them suffered from serious loss of memory and took to heading outdoors at any time of the day or night. At age fourteen, Rebecca was appointed to be their live-in carer – no mean task for a youngster.

I recall my Granny speaking in Gaelic of Rebecca, and saying she was a wise child. Seoras Ross, by the way, was a devout Christian, a Godly man. In course of time, our first-born son was called after him. I give thanks that much of the quality of the first Seoras followed through into the next.

* * *

Back to the romance. At first, our meetings took place at village hall dances and I graduated to seeing her home afterwards. Rebecca became employed as an unqualified teacher in a tiny one-family school on the little island, Isle Martin, just opposite Ardmair Beach some four miles out of Ullapool. Her six pupils, the Boa family, had a marvellous life both in and out of school.

The road from Ullapool to Ardmair was as rough as the proverbial bag of nails, with long steep gradients. Daily, for several years, come rain hail sleet or snow, Rebecca cycled the route twice daily, and if she woke to find a punctured bike tyre, she walked, then as usual, completing her journey by motor launch. Happily, her return home often coincided with my return from my school car trip, and eagerly I would stop and take her and her bike into the old *Austin*.

Life of course is full of change and she started work in the one and only Ullapool bank, her workstation facing a window looking right onto Argyle Street, along which I often drove vehicles. She started acknowledging me with a discreet little hand wave, and my, how that lifted my heart. I probably drove towards the bank more often than was strictly necessary. An unspoken understanding grew between us and we were definitely 'in love'.

* * *

As my love-saturated mind began to consider the way ahead, it soon became obvious that from a financial aspect, Rebecca and I would never be able to marry and set up house on my current earnings. My long time boyhood friend, Martin Hill, had already gone in for civil engineering and was based in Glasgow. I think in Easter 1951, he holidayed with me in Ullapool. He impressed upon me the wonderful life in Glasgow. He was saying, "Why don't you come and work in Glasgow? There's room in my digs, and Kate, my Irish landlady, is pressing me to find another lodger for her. It's not economical for her having just one."

But where would I work? "No problem," said Martin, "my friend Bobby Breen works in a small civil engineering firm, I'll get him to speak to their plant manager, John Lockerbie, and I'm sure he'll take you on as a plant fitter.

Chapter 8

Glasgow, Marriage and a New Life.

I felt strongly, that if I was going to get anywhere, I had to break out of my present dead-end situation. I was also becoming more and more aware of Ullapool's alcoholic hazards of that time. An interview was arranged, John Lockerbie was impressed enough to nod his head and give me 'The Start' as they called it, and for about 50% more money than my Ullapool £5. Poor man, I suspect that if he had properly understood the limitations of my knowledge and experience, the outcome might have been different. However, I believe that, at the end of the day, he got his pound of flesh, and both the company, *A.M. Tweedie Ltd,* and I benefited – I, by the skills learned and experience gained, Tweedie's, by a level of conscientiousness and productivity well above their norm.

I think that in my favour had been the fact that in his younger days, John Lockerbie and his pals had camped at Ullapool and he obviously had fond memories of the local talent.

Did I know Cathie who had blond hair? Yes, of course I did. In Ullapool everyone knew everyone else. Now middle-aged and with two small children, John's life wasn't so carefree as in single days.

* * *

I hastened back to Ullapool and gave Uncle M appropriate notice. He didn't seem much surprised. Thereafter, I drew most of my sparse P.O. Savings; at Inverness, I purchased a complete new tool kit and headed south on the old steam train. By arrangement, Martin Hill met me at what used to be Buchanan St. railway station. Irish widow Kate made me warmly welcome; my new life had begun and, soon, love letters started to flow between Rebecca and me.

As soon as the winter session of night classes started, I enrolled to study mechanical engineering, which although focussing essentially on marine steam applications, has stood me in good stead.

Second-hand boiler suit and tackety boots from ' *The Barras*' and a few mornings later, I hauled my heavy tool kit onto a tram car and got halfway to *Tweedie's*. The remaining mile or so I walked, with wrists aching.

I was allocated my first job, an ancient road roller, its gearbox a great big cast iron box, with no lid and empty. Along with it, I received a strong wooden box containing a mixture of shafts, gears, brass washers, etc., some old some new. By common logic and the grace of God, over a couple of days, I managed to sort out the parts and, as it turned out, happily assemble them in their correct positions.

My next hurdle was to fit new steering kingpins and bushes to an old *International* truck. The bore of the bushes was undersize and they had to be enlarged to the correct fit using an expanding reamer. I had never heard of an expanding reamer, never mind use one. Again by the grace of God, I managed to figure things out and make the *International* roadworthy.

Most of my colleagues were mainly worldly wise, time served men, and I think there was some interest in what capabilities I, as a country yokel, might have. In the providence of God, my rating got a good lift one day. The firm's tipper fleet were all *Fords* and, like all commercial vehicles of the time, their tyres were held on the wheels by a detachable rim. All that I had ever encountered elsewhere were 'split' rims, and with a bit of practice, I learned to fit them easily enough – like a piece of steel rope into a groove on the wheel.

Ford rims, however, were not split and quite another matter. Normally, all the tyre work was farmed out to a specialist tyre company. For some reason, the workshop's top man, also son of the foreman, was given the task of fitting a new tyre to a *Ford* wheel, and he just couldn't do it. He wrestled and sweated and cursed unsuccessfully; everybody in the place had a go and were defeated, but didn't leave the scene. Watching all this from the corner of my eye, I felt fairly sure I could do the necessary. I didn't want to appear to be a 'smart Alex' and possibly a failed one at that, but I took the plunge. I walked across and asked Percy if I could try. Willingly the tyre levers were passed to me and within half a minute the rim snapped into place. I handed the levers back and returned to my job leaving several open mouths.

In approaching mechanical problems, I found that the city boys didn't have the cool logical reasoning of the 'country loon'.

Great would have been their tittle-tattle had they been privy to a boob I committed about that time, and probably I would have been consequently 'looking for a job'. I had been trusted with the overhaul of a *Ford V8* engine, smooth running, but nasty things to overhaul. For the first time in my life, I had to fit new piston rings to pistons. In my ignorance, I placed the first piston in the bench vice and wound the vice closed. To my horror, the precision and expensive piston ceased to be round and became oval. My grey matter churning wildly, I quickly released the vice, turned the piston 90 degrees and tightened the vice till the original shape was near enough restored, the while, sweating and hoping against hope that nobody had seen the incident. In due time, the engine seemed to run well and there were no repercussions. Combustion engine pistons I might say are accurate to within a thousand's part of an inch!

Eventually my rating became so high that I always got the directors' cars to do.

Today, the working conditions in that workshop would have created a national scandal. Low roof, walls that had at one time been white washed and the concrete floor thickly encrusted with a mixture of grease, tar and mud. Round the walls there were continuous heavy wooden benches with great heavy tool drawers.

One day, I opened my drawer and a large surprised rat within met my surprised gaze from without. It turned to escape over the back of the drawer, but was just too slow, and by sharply thrusting my weight down on the front of the drawer, I successfully 'nailed' it between the drawer end and the under side of the bench, thus ending its days.

The premises were infested with the creatures, which were really an overspill from an equally dingy sweet factory straight across the road from us. My taste for sweet things was not affected then, or since.

All contractors' plant units of any size had diesel engines, all of which were hand-started, even sizeable crawler excavators. Diesel engines of the time were reluctant starters from cold; nowadays, they have lots of built in starting aids. Then, the only aid was a flaming firebrand held beside the engine air intake, which as the engine was manually 'swung', sucked in the flames and did the necessary. Not many of my colleagues were robust enough for the swing bit, and after they had had a few unsuccessful attempts, and saturated the cylinders with unburned diesel fuel, there would often be a call, "Hector, come and give me a swing." I'd been blessed with physical stature and strength, so usually it was a first go start, whereupon the engine sent out clouds of thick black choking smoke till you couldn't see across the workshop. As the revs slowly built up, the smoke gradually reduced till the exhaust ran 'clean'.

My successes were good for my prestige, but probably not for my ego, nor the lungs of anyone present.

Tweedie's were awarded a contract in Stornoway that required the use of a *Ruston Bucyrus* crawler excavator. Stornoway had no 'Ro-Ro' (Roll on, Roll off) facilities then. Heavy items being landed had to be hoisted ashore by a land-based crane with a maximum lift of five tons – and the *Ruston* weighed probably three times that. Defying geographical logic, it was to be shipped from Leith to Stornoway.

The workshop foreman, old Percy, was appointed to travel to Leith to completely dismantle the Ruston at the docks, and later, to rebuild it at Stornoway. I was happily surprised when he invited me to be his assistant and drive him daily between Glasgow and Leith. The Glasgow to Edinburgh road was then a lethal three-lane carriageway, the scene of frequent fatal accidents, as vehicles from opposite directions met disastrously in the central overtaking lane.

Growing old, I suspect Percy wasn't keen to be driving on it. In fact some eighteen months later, he managed to get himself killed while driving a works' van.

Dismantling of the *Ruston* was carried out to virtually the last nut and bolt. As we kept chucking the 'thousand' bits and pieces into various boxes and buckets, I expressed my concern that we should try to keep some recognisable order to them, whereupon Percy with a wicked grin grabbed a well-filled bucket and shook it all up as though to get a good mix. He knew every nut and bolt and exactly where each should go. It would be about a couple of years later before I, too, had such knowledge of the many types of machine on which I worked.

The summer of 1951 was one of beautiful sunshine. To my delight, our summer holidays came round, the whole firm would close down for the week of the 'Glasgow Fair'.

Work stopped at noon on Saturday, and armed with my case containing holiday clothes, I high-tailed it to catch the one o'clock train from Buchanan St. station for Inverness en route to Ullapool. The station was thronged with people as Glasgow emptied itself for the 'Fair'. Although eagerly looked forward to, the 'Fair' could be something of an ordeal for some. There is the tale of the perspiring dad of a large family mopping his brow as he finally got them settled into a carriage compartment, muttering, "My _ _ _, I'll be glad when this fair is over." Along with this 'generous' holiday, we also had one day at New Year and I think one at Easter.

Gradually, conditions in construction work improved; Christmas Day became a holiday, followed by other additional holidays, till eventually it seemed to me that a halt should be called to the extras. By the time I finished, it was two weeks for summer, two weeks for Christmas/New Year, a week at Easter plus other odd days, free overalls and laundry, boots hats and gloves. It reminds me of the day in *Tweedie's* when I went to the store and asked for a pair of work gloves (returnable by the way). The stores boss asked me why I wanted them. I explained that John Lockerbie had asked me to go and sort out a bundle of jagged steel ropes; they were sprouting a profusion of broken wire strands; we called them 'hairy' ropes.

Davie of the stores was exceedingly reluctant, as the gloves 'might get spoiled', and he wasn't kidding! After a bit of haggle and the go ahead from John Lockerbie, he relented.

I cannot leave the *Tweedie* scene without recounting the tale of 'the blind dog and the silver paper'. Tea breaks took place around a small round solid fuel stove, which also served to boil up an urn of water for our brew. Every man had his own 'billy can', smoke-blackened and with a wire handle; a pack lunch from home or 'digs' (lodgings) completed his repast. Many and varied were the subjects aired around the stove. You need to know that people collected silver foil from cigarette packets to give to charity organisations that got money for it.

One charity was 'Guide Dogs for the Blind'.

As you will see, even then, not everybody knew. A visiting lorry driver opened a new pack of cigarettes and chucked the silver foil into the ashes of the fire. A voice said, "Don't do that, I'm collecting it."

Lorry driver: "What do you want it for?"

First voice: "For a blin dug (blind dog)."

Lorry driver: "Whit's the dug gonny dae wi silver paper? (What's the dog going to do with silver paper?)"

And, like the store man, he wasn't kidding either!

* * *

Love letters continued to flow back and forth between Ullapool and Glasgow, steadily growing in warmth and urgency.

Telephones were not all that commonly used by working people and mobiles hadn't even been imagined. Then a letter arrived from Rebecca, saying she would be coming to stay with her Aunt Joe in Glasgow for a week at Easter. Aunt Joe lived in Strathbungo, a district within walking distance of Minard Road in Shawlands where I lived. To say I was delighted would be an understatement.

I met her off the train, the weather was glorious all week and life in the famous words of Parahandy was 'chust sublime'.

Queen's Park, resplendent in the sunshine just across the road from Aunt Joe's, was well suited to the 'sweet nothings' of lovers, and also for old men and children sailing their vessels in the large boating pond. In addition to the sweet nothings, that week I bought a ring and we became officially engaged to marry; plans for a wedding in July (1952) started to be laid.

All too soon our wonder week came to an end and dear Rebecca departed north. I had some difficulty taking aboard that in a matter of weeks I would become a married man.

* * *

The appointed day arrived and on the 22nd of July 1952, we were married by the Rev. Matheson in the basement hall of St Jude's Free Presbyterian church in Glasgow – as I recall, an occasion of grave solemnity from start to finish. The formalities completed, we moved to the Burlington House Hotel on Bath St. for the reception.

I expect there are other elements of the day, which should have been given higher attention in my mind, but fifty-one years later, I still can't forget the amazing cost of transport for our wedding party from church to hotel. The journey wouldn't take more than 15 minutes, nevertheless, from *Travel Trips Ltd*, for the guests we had a *Silver Roadways* luxury coach for the princely sum of 10 shillings (50p). The receipt is still among my souvenirs. .

Marriage to Rebecca, Glasgow, July 1952

For ourselves, the happy couple, we had a *Rolls Royce* limousine for exactly the same price, but even at that, our tiny 'kitty' was feeling stress

In the weeks before the wedding, there had been feverish pavement pounding in search of living quarters. These I finally found at 16 Camphill Avenue, a handsome Victorian terrace house close to Queen's Park and near Langside monument, commemorating Mary Queen of Scot's battle there. The house was owner-occupied by a family, the top floor rented to Miss McIndoe, sister of Sir Archibald McIndoe, pioneer of plastic surgery for burned RAF aircrew of WW2. For £1.50 a week we rented the sub-basement flat. We had a lovely big sitting room, unfurnished but for a threadbare carpet, one grotty armchair and a sideboard, a tiny bedroom, a tinier kitchen, with ancient gas cooker and a sink, which also had to serve for daily personal hygiene and finally a 'reverse in' loo under the stair. Once a week, we could each have a bath upstairs on an allotted night. We managed a new double bed on the never-never and Rebecca was most resourceful at the Glasgow 'Barras' (barrows, street market) where she picked up a comfortable old armchair and other bits and pieces to make our home. She thoroughly enjoyed raking the barras and for the purpose, wore a specially decrepit raincoat. She was much amused one day when a would-be customer mistook her for a stall owner and asked her the price of an item.

At Glasgow's Charings Cross stood the *Grande Hotel*, there I had booked our first married night's accommodation, a closely guarded secret. However my tight security turned out to be poor order; as we were in the middle of dressing next morning, I answered a knock on our bedroom door. To my surprise, there was a pageboy, bearing a telegram addressed to Mr. & Mrs. Mackenzie, Newly Weds etc. The message was brief, with no senders name; it just said: 'AIN'T LOVE GRANDE'.

Next night was spent in Ardrossan and the following morning we crossed the sea for a very pleasant week at *Laag Hotel*, complete with its open-air palm trees, in the south-west of the island of Arran. One week later, we returned to our semi-basement with just about enough money for food till my next pay-day. Thirty something years later, Rebecca and I on a motor-cycling camping holiday had dinner in *Laag Hotel*. Having foolishly told the waitress of our previous stay, we were treated to a free bottle of wine, and somewhat to our embarrassment, the focus of attention of all in the well-filled dining room.

After three years in *Tweedie's*, I changed jobs. I moved to *Sandy Gilmour (Plant) Ltd*. Curiously, I replaced one, Alex Blue, who went to the place I had vacated at *Tweedie's*.

Chapter 9

Sandy Gilmour's

*S*andy Gilmour owned and ran his lucrative little business with efficiency and dedication. 'We carry no passengers'. 'Nothing is too good for my machines'. There was a plant manager-cum-salesman, a secretary-cum-tea lady, one other fitter, a stores-cum-delivery man and machine operators as necessary.

Through selling lubricating oil to farmers, Sandy had become creditor to a farmer who couldn't pay. Settlement was agreed by the handing over of one crawler bulldozer and an ex-Army *Scammell* machinery carrier. This 'monster' had obviously been built to economy standard for the British Army. It had a wooden cab, no front brakes, and a fearsome crash gate-change gearbox with six speeds. The driver's seat was offset from its large steering wheel and foot pedals. It was articulated and pulled a long semi-low trailer. There was no power steering or cab heater and the cab had copious 'cooling' drafts. It required a hardy, strong and patient driver. On up-changes the heavy fly-wheeled *Gardner* engine took an age between gears to drop revs sufficiently for the next gear to be engaged. Its regular driver, Dougie, was a pipe smoker; he could comfortably light up during the pause. On the couple of occasions I drove it through the city, I found that all other traffic gave it a wide berth, and clear road opened before it like magic.

I found Sandy to be a generous employer of few words. He expected full effort and honesty. When he didn't get them, there would be an extra week's wages next payday and a curt, "We'll not need you on Monday." He found in Glasgow Corporation a willing and continuing customer to hire his bulldozer. The Corporation had started the development of large new housing estates – Castlemilk, Drumchapel, Easterhouse and a string of smaller ones.

The plant hire business was money for old rope in those days. When I arrived, the fleet had built up to six machines and the old *Scammell* was getting plenty business, too.

Suddenly the one other fitter vanished from the scene and so did a large quantity of expensive new tools from Sandy's private garage.

The fleet continued to grow in numbers and with ever bigger and more expensive machines. Two more fitters were engaged. One Saturday, Sandy quietly told me the place needed a foreman; a new one would be starting on Monday.

"It should really be you, Hector, but you're not enough of a bastard. You'll get a pay increase."

The new foreman was strong and active, but soon departed due to a drunken spree with a company vehicle.

"Hector, will you run things in the meantime...", which lasted long enough to see a move into much larger premises in open fields at Summerstone, just beyond Lambhill and the city boundary.

* * *

An enthusiastic colleague had persuaded me to buy a car from a small garage in Bishopbriggs - an early 1930s *B.S.A.* three-wheeled sporty two-seater, with a cream coloured body, a narrow red body stripe, and soft top. It cost £15 and the body was in questionable condition. I must have been mad to buy it.

Nevertheless, holiday time came and one evening with open top, Rebecca and I set off for Ullapool, via Glencoe. We were going well when suddenly the engine started to stammer and stutter and we just managed to stagger into a garage at Balloch, where I had to fork out £8 for a new battery, making a sizeable hole in my sparse holiday money, but the B.S.A. got a new lease of life.

I had noticed that the (external) radiator cap had a hole in the centre where probably some fancy mascot had been mounted in better days. As we soared up the ascent of the Black Mount, without warning, a jet of hot water spouted from the hole, liberally

109

showering us. With well over 100 miles to go, it was not a good omen. As the weather roughened, I pulled in and raised the tatty soft hood, and set off again. Then Rebecca's door opened of its own accord and, thereafter, would not stay closed. She continued the journey holding it with her hand, but with no complaint. Every now and again the radiator spouted like a whale, but now we had some cover.

As we motored on – into darkness, over Rannoch Moor and headed for *King's House* – the wind started to rise. Squalls of rain joined our spouting radiator and suddenly Rebecca's side of the soft roof broke loose, yawning wide to the driving rain. She grabbed it with her spare hand and hauled it down into place, but it would not stay. So we continued our journey, Rebecca with one hand holding the roof, the other holding her door, and still never a word of complaint. We were more like a ship in a storm than a motorcar.

Descending to low ground and Glencoe village, the weather eased and by the grace of God we reached Inverness for a break, wash and breakfast before continuing to Ullapool. Like most successful adventures, we could look back on it with a degree of amusement and accomplishment.

* * *

I must record one of the number of occasions I believe God rescued me from serious accident.

From time to time, the bulldozer engines needed major overhauls. The process entailed taking the heavy cylinder block across the city to an engineering machine shop in our light pickup truck. One bright summer day, unusually there were two to go and with more enthusiasm than wisdom, I decided to take them both in one trip. The route went over a sharp little hill at Prospecthill Rd. Gathering speed I went over the brow of the hill, and right in my path, a heavily laden tipper truck was toiling up towards me on my side of the road while a parked direct-sales grocery van, a happy housewife shopping at its open rear door, was blocking the other lane.

B.S.A. Three-wheeler

On auto-pilot, I applied full emergency stop measures and the grossly overloaded pickup took not the slightest notice. To my right was a high stone kerb and pedestrian pavement, behind the pavement, continuous garden fence and hedges, and a sturdy iron lighting pole on the edge of the pavement. I got a glimpse of astonished faces of housewife and van man as I shot the pickup over the kerb and between the lighting pole and the housewife's garden fence, marvelling that there had been enough space – and I assure you nothing to spare. Regaining the now empty road in front, I continued as if nothing had transpired and very 'shook up'.

I gradually regained control for a 'Halt' sign ahead. The remainder of my journey was with extreme care. From then on it was one engine block at a time.

* * *

After five years in our rented accommodation, Rebecca said she had seen a flat advertised and doing sums, she thought we could afford to buy it with a mortgage. As children, she and her brother had been talked into signing away a property inheritance and she was determined that one day she would have a house of her own. We went for it and became the owners of a six room and kitchen flat, two up, in a row of magnificent red sandstone terrace houses on the high part of Wilton Street.

For the benefit of family readers, Wilton St. runs from Queen Margaret Drive, over a sharp hill and down to Maryhill Rd (all in Glasgow).

Our Victorian flat was from another era and built to a superb standard. The wall skirtings of thick dark wood with rounded top were a foot high. Heavy panelled doors led into two large 'public' rooms, a master bedroom, three smaller bedrooms, a bathroom and a large kitchen. We set about furnishing it with good quality second hand furniture.

In the Book of the *Proverbs* of King Solomon, the last chapter tells of the qualities of a virtuous woman. It says, 'she does not eat the bread of idleness'; Rebecca certainly matched up. Quickly, she had an ad in *The Scotsman* and taken in three boarders from the nearby hospital and the university – a young surgeon and two lecturers, and at last we started to make a bit of money.

I advertised and sold the *B.S.A.* for £45. Soon we were able to buy a new 175 cc *Lambretta* scooter, our 'family' transport, which gave us new liberty and mobility.

Popular Saturday trips took us up the 'Rest and be Thankful' and, via Lochgoilhead, to Carrick Castle (Argyllshire) where an old school friend had a hotel and pub. The road ended at Carrick Castle, a really quiet spot, but John Mackenzie said he made sufficient money from his regular *Glasgow Fair* pub clients to keep his business afloat all year. Our trusty *Lambretta* even took us on an overnight run to Ullapool for the Easter holiday. I can still feel the hailstones rattling on my helmet as we battered through Glencoe. We drove into Ullapool at 7 a.m. next morning – a marvellous trip!

* * *

At the new premises Sandy G. did well by his men. There was a new minibus to take the staff to and from the city centre, a benefit almost unheard of then, also a canteen, the catering done by a live-in caretaker couple. Mrs. B. had spent many years cooking for aristocracy and she was an expert. When one of our 'ruffians' would compliment her on some special production, her usual response would be, "Ay, Sir Archie was fond o' that one."

Sandy was a ferocious driver; he indulged himself in fast up-market cars and he didn't have to worry how he treated them. He had a new employee at the town office, Mr. Robertson, a sedate retired tea planter. Mr. Robertson was taken for a tour of the new works. On the way back to town at high speed, as they approached a narrow hump backed bridge over a canal, it became apparent that the passenger's feet were being pressed very hard on the car floor. Sandy said to him, "Mr. Robertson, the pedals are on my side."

On a late night return home, his *Jaguar* had sustained some pretty unsightly damage to its front 'wing'. The bruised and battered area soon rusted and one day his wife noticed me looking at it.

"Ah," she said, "it's getting worn, Hector...he's needing a new one." She was talking about the eighteen-month-old *Jaguar*, not the 'wing'.

* * *

One day, Sandy told me the firm needed a plant inspector and it would be me. "A new van will be delivered tomorrow...just use it as your own and fill up on our account. I want a written report on each machine every two weeks."

Now there were 50-60 machines scattered over the whole south of Scotland, many in remote locations – I became a very busy lad.

Soon, my journeys were taking me as far south as Leeds. In my first year, I covered over 35,000 miles in my snappy new *Morris Minor*. It could achieve 70 mph and mostly, of necessity, did. In addition to reports, I was also required to carry out whatever running repairs I could manage within two or three hours, 'But don't get tied down on a job'.

Each year, my annual mileage and earnings increased. The boarder business went so well that Rebecca set her sights and ambitions higher. She announced that there was a bungalow for sale in Bearsden.

"Could we go and see it?"

Bearsden was decidedly up-market; I thought, beyond our resources. Rebecca was not to be put off and see it we did. We found a little old lady in an ivy-covered bungalow, with a beautiful garden, and she showed us round with enthusiasm. The sale was for offers over £3,000, but on a second visit, she told us she liked us and wanted us to have it. She had received higher offers, but from us she would accept £3000. After three years in Wilton Street, we sold up and with our finances stretched to the limit – probably slightly beyond it – we moved into No.5 Lochend Drive, Bearsden..

Ten years of married life had elapsed when Rebecca suddenly announced pregnancy. On the tenth of March 1963, a Sunday morning, I was at work when the telephone rang, and I heard that our firstborn, Seoras, had arrived. It was a euphoric point in my life. I felt something bordering on levitation. I hurried to the nursing home in Helensburgh where he was born. He had only weighed in at 3lb 10ozs, but he has proved that good stuff comes in small parcels.

Fact is indeed stranger than fiction. My first instant impression of the tiny face in an incubator immediately brought to my mind my late grandmother who had died years before in her eighties.

Our bungalow at Bearsden dated back to the 1920s and was therefore of a quality that subsequent builders found uneconomical to produce. To the rear it had a large sunny garden, surrounded by tall privet hedging and accessed through a broad privet arch. In addition to flower areas and a big lawn, there was a well stocked raised rockery with a small open area inside it – soon turned into a sandpit, where a small boy (or two) could while away pleasant hours before life's responsibilities started to move in on them.

Seoras at Bearsden
1964

It was as Seoras's little pal, David, arrived one morning that the following conversation was overheard.

"Hello Seoras...my granny died."

"Did she?"

"Yes...she's away to heaven."

Then correction came, "Well she's not away yet, but she's going at two o'clock."

* * *

At the end of one year, my *Morris Minor* van was replaced with a new *Morris Minor Traveller*, the small estate car version. These little cars were very special. With their external body framework of varnished ash wood, they were good-looking, economical to buy and to run, and would happily gobble the miles all day every day if required, with never a moment's trouble. To add to efficiency, two-way radio had been installed, something of a novelty then.

* * *

We enjoyed a period of special bliss, happy marriage, nice home, a little boy and an income to cover our needs. In March 1965, our second son was born. Rebecca's mother (Granny) was staying with us for the occasion and to look after Seoras. We had already decided the baby would be called Hector.

Hector lived just one day. It was the most traumatic experience of my life when on Sunday morning the telephone rang and the voice at the other end told me the baby had died. I hurried down to *Redlands* nursing home to see Rebecca and speechless, we wept together till there were no more tears. In a state of shock, I drove home to my bewildered mother-in-law and her little charge.

I quietly picked up a towel and my swimming trunks and drove to Maryhill baths, where I swam length after length till I could swim no more. How little we know of what's happening to each other and not one of the many assorted beings at Maryhill baths would have the slightest idea of the turmoil going on in my head that morning.

A little funeral service was arranged at Hillfoot cemetery, Bearsden. On reflection, how wonderful it was that we already had a church connection. The Minister, the Rev. Hector Cameron (originally from Resolis in the Black Isle) was everything one could wish for – quiet, comforting, and practical. The only others attending were my brother-in-law, Sulan, from Ullapool and Rebecca's cousin, Rev. Alaister Ross.

The grave, with a white marble stone, lies close to the gate at Hillfoot cemetery in Bearsden. Somewhere along the line, we had been invited to attend services at our nearby Drumchapel Free Church of Scotland, and I was becoming more and more interested in the content of the preaching and of the Bible.

'Weeping may endure for a night, but joy cometh in the morning'
(Psalm 30:5)

On April 6th 1967, a little boy, Kenneth Lachie Mackenzie, was born to us. As a little boy, women openly said they would like to steal him, and to this day, although now grown up, married and a dad himself, people will spontaneously say to me 'everybody loves Kenny'.

The Rev Angus MacInnes, Minister of the Church of Scotland on Bothwell St. lived across the road from us, and on a Sunday morning when his service was to be broadcast on the BBC, he invited us to come along. We were installed in the front pew, close to a microphone, where Kenny soon fell asleep and, unusually, snored powerfully, thus it was that he has the distinction of snoring on the BBC aged about 18 months.

Seoras and new brother Kenny, 1967

Chapter 10

The Muck Shifters.

*I*n civil engineering circles, the reshaping of sites in preparation for building or other reasons is referred to as 'earth-moving', but among those who actually did the moving, they spoke of 'muck-shifting'. Imagine the consternation and total disbelief of the lady at the news agents the day Rebecca asked her to please order up 'The Muck-shifter' magazine for her. She was amazed to learn that there was indeed such a publication. For a number of years I was a regular and avid reader.

My roving commission in *Sandy G's* took me as far north as Wester Ross and south to Yeadon airport serving Leeds and surrounding area. I was lapping up the variety of sites, scenes, machines and personalities I encountered.

* * *

My new *Morris Minor Traveller* estate car was mostly driven near to its limit on the twisted west highland roads, gobbling up the miles like nobody's business. It happened that a successful contractor of the time had got himself a new *Aston Martin* car, and to show it off, took Sandy on a trip to West Loch Tarbert in Argyllshire where there was a *Sandy* machine on his road contract. On his return, Sandy told me how fast the *Aston* was and their remarkably short journey time from Glasgow. It was a regular route of mine en route to Campbeltown, but I thought it best not to reveal that I was doing it quicker in my *Traveller*.

As *Sandy's* fleet continued to grow, I visited expanding airports, dam sites, steel works, coal mines and burning waste bings, reservoirs, building and demolition sites, oil refineries and even an ocean terminal.

The latter at Finart on Loch Long provided a couple of amusing incidents.

Towards the end of a day, a *Caterpillar* machine at Finart had suffered a broken exhaust manifold from falling rock, and I was called on to 'do something' to get it going for the morning start at 8 a.m.

There was no new part available.

I had dinner and invited Rebecca along for the run. I found the machine under cover in a large workshop. The cast iron manifold was in half a dozen fragments. Cast iron can be tricky stuff to weld. It really calls for a properly trained welder, which I certainly wasn't. *Sandy's* plant was renowned for reliability; and every effort had to be made to restore it for the morning.

I laboriously filed each part into shape and successfully 'jigsawed' them into place with oxy-acetylene brazing. As I was refitting the manifold, the night watchman entered and his eyes were popping as he saw a pretty, tweed-coated young lady standing on the *Caterpillar's* track and leaning across the engine with a spanner in her hand; she was in the act of handing it over to me, out of his sight behind the engine.

* * *

Finart was an oil tanker terminal capable of taking the largest vessels at any state of the tide. Oil was pumped by pipeline straight across Scotland to the large refinery at Grangemouth. Tankers could tie up at its shoreline quay, which had 90 feet minimum depth at the lowest tide. It was said to be the only port in Europe with such capability.

A colleague of mine on an evening visit was in its 'state of the art' harbour office. The duty Harbour Master, a Lewis-man who, like many of his fellow islanders, was just about born with the sea in his veins and deceptively laid back, was in radio contact with a 'distressed' American super tanker in the Bay of Biscay. The tanker had been in a storm and lost an anchor vital to its berthing at the other side of the Atlantic. The American, perhaps not unnaturally, was a bit up tight and demanding to know when high tide would be in Loch Long, as he must come in and get a new anchor.

His state of tension was not improved as 'Lewis' told him, "Ach, it will not matter, just come in any time."

The response was along the lines, "Listen, Bud, this is a LOADED SUPER TANKER...we draw 60 feet of water...blah...blah...bla..."

Lewis: "It will be all right, just you come in."

The poor American was being mercilessly wound up while 'Lewis' remained sublimely unruffled.

* * *

Sandy Gilmour's was a time of numerous adventures and marvellous characters. Sam Moore was a fitter who later went on to have his own plant hire business. He and I had just overhauled the clutch on a particularly big bulldozer on an 'open cast' coal site in Ayrshire. The machine had a peculiar dual voltage battery system and Sam had repeatedly tried to make the correct battery connections. They were extra large capacity batteries and when you get the connections wrong, there is a violent blue flash and bang. Sam was making what he hoped was his final and this time correct connection, when just at the crucial moment, without warning a large explosive charge was fired in the workings below us, out of our sight, but not so far away. If it were possible for a human to have kittens, they would have been instantly produced.

* * *

About this time in the mid 1950s, Glasgow and the industrial belt had the worst 'pea-souper' fogs I've ever experienced. With visibility close to zero, Rebecca and I were on our *Lambretta* heading for Bearsden, and even with the street lighting on, it was impossible to see from one street lamp to the next. At walking pace, I literally hugged the kerb, struggling to keep a mental note of my exact location by the street corners passed - otherwise we would have had no idea where we were. Similarly, if you wandered even a yard from the kerb, you lost it, because it was only possible to see 3 or 4 feet of tarmac road – position and direction anybody's guess. Added to that there was the hazard of oncoming traffic just as blind as oneself.

Again, Sam Moore and I were returning one evening from a job in the Falkirk area, when we hit the fog somewhere east of Glasgow. It quickly thickened to impossibility. Sam did the driving while I stood up behind the cab of our *Landrover* pickup With the back sliding window open and peering into the thick grey, I navigated in the fashion of an old time bomb aimer with verbal …left…left…right…left. Sam could see literally nothing.

We made it to our depot to unload our heavy gear, then headed through the city towards Sam's home. We knew there was a large demolished city block site in the Springburn area where it would be safe to drop him off. As Sam stopped the *Landrover*, I looked and was amazed to see a long line of vehicles pulled up behind us and stretching into the gloom. Probably with faith in the *Landrover's* 'navigator', they had doggedly followed us up over the kerb and pavement and onto the waste ground.

I hadn't gone far on my way home when I came upon an 'artic' road tanker, its half demolished front end buried in the rear end of a stationary tramcar.

* * *

The characters of the muck shifting world were an absolute delight and would merit a book to themselves. I salute them everyone: Joe Strachan, Dave Beveridge, Dozer O'Donald, Willie Bennie, John Friary, John McQuade, John (Darkie) McBride and many others. They worked hard, some drank hard, but all would have given you their last shilling.

I had been called on the radio to look in at a bulldozer 'bogged' in the duck pond in Glasgow's Queen's Park. The machine had been engaged in cleaning out the pond, when it lost traction some way from the bank. It was a sizeable pond, surrounded by trees; the ducks had departed, the water now a thick mud porridge (slurry), and marginally less than wellie depth. There was a second 'rescue' machine, standing on the bank, but no machine operators present.

I called on the radio for a spare operator and while I waited for his arrival, I got the second machine into position in the pond for a tow out. A heavy wire sling had already been provided, and wearing my tall wellies, I coupled the two drawbars together and pulled the sling taut. It finished up just out of sight about an inch under the mud. I then discovered that I could stand comfortably on the thick sling, probably with a toe just touching a drawbar for balance, but apparently unsupported. That is how Joe Strachan saw me when he arrived on the bank. I called him over to operate the rescue machine. There was a long pause and then in shaky tones he said, "Hector, how are you doing that?"

He obviously thought I was walking on the water (slurry).

Dave Beveridge was a handsome young man from the Borders. A real gentleman, he worked a lot in remote forestry areas. If his machine was stationary and the engine running, curious deer would come right up to it, but the moment he stopped the engine they took off at speed. On one occasion, using old fence wire, he actually snared a deer.

Another time, I visited him whilst he had been working in a quarry excavating material for the formation of a bund wall going out into the Firth of Forth. It was a freezing day with a biting wind. (In those days machine operators worked in the open – no cabs – they were hardy, they had to be.) From his duffle coat pocket, Dave produced a few pieces of what looked like fossilised tree bark. It was of distinct diamond shape, a type I had only ever seen in impressions of pre-history.

"Hector, will you take these back to Glasgow with you and give them to an 'ologist (sic) to see what he thinks of them."

His nose was emitting horizontal streamers in the freezing wind (as was mine) and he reached into his other pocket to withdraw an old sock to use in place of the handkerchief, which he hadn't got.

I never did hear the 'ologist's' verdict.

* * *

Dozer (Danny) O'Donald from Donegal has to be mentioned. He was the life and soul in whatever company he happened to be. It was often hard to know whether his remarks and observations were deliberate witticisms or just a natural aptitude for odd forms of words. There was the occasion when, aggrieved at our plant engineer, he said to me, "Hector, it's terrible the lies that man is telling, and not a word of truth in them."

Coming into our depot tearoom one day, he announced, "Boys, I've just bought a farm back home."

Asked what size it was, he replied, "Well, there's terty (thirty) acres when the tide is in and tree (three) hundred when it's out."

One night after visiting Dozer and his machine, I had an overnight stay at Yeadon in England where he was engaged in runway extension work at Leeds and Bradford airport.

'Dozer' O'Donald 'muck shifting' for a NATO refuelling depot at Campbeltown Loch ~ 1960s

Danny had always had a keen interest in flying. In the evening as we socialised over a 'pint', he was relating to me how he had got to know the boss of the local flying club.

"I asked him about the flying...Sure, there's nothing to it, Hector...there are no halt signs or any of that stuff. He was very interested in my *D8* (*Caterpillar*), but it's amazing how tick (thick) a man like that could be – I could not get him to understand how the turbocharger worked, and how it was the shteam (steam) that made it go."

For the non-technical, of course it is nothing of the kind, it is driven by the engine exhaust gasses.

Willie Bennie was an immaculate loner, an expert with his machine, which he kept as immaculate as himself. He even bought expensive car polish out of his own pocket, and gave his *Caterpillar* a showroom shine that few even attempted to match.

Earth-moving sites, where heavy machinery is in use, can be very difficult to negotiate on foot. With the continuous roar of un-silenced engines and heavy mud with foot deep ruts, as machines roar back and forth, a high level of alertness is required, to stay in one piece.

Willie Bennie had been working somewhere in the Northampton area when his machine 'threw' a track. As he hurried on foot for assistance, a passing monster trailing a wire sling caught his foot and all but severed it from his leg. Sinews were the only remaining connection. Somehow, the surgeons managed to clean him up and tie it all together again.

He had a brother in the area doing well with his own plant business. As Willie was starting to recover in hospital and feel a bit perky again, he decided to telephone 'oor Dave'. I understand the conversation went something like this:

"Dave, I thought at least you would have come to see me."

"Ah well, Willie," was the reply, "I was waiting till you were more serious."

* * *

124

I first met John Friary at Glasgow's Drumchapel housing site, when not a single house had yet been built. His machine had suffered a major breakdown. Ronnie, a Glaswegian, and I had been sent to put things right. We had been squatting down dismantling the track drive system where a collapsed bearing had badly torn the heavy drive support shaft that passes right through the rear of the machine. This shaft is seldom removed and is often rusted and seized in its location and can be very difficult to dislodge. John Friary, the operator, was a tall thin bespectacled Irishman who turned out to be probably the strongest man I had ever met.

The site tea hooter sounded and men streamed towards the tea huts. Ronnie rose and was wiping his hands when John spoke, "And where do you think you're going?"

"I'm going for my tea, John."

"You get back down where you were, I'll bring you your tea," in tones which produced a quiet 'yes, John'.

The tea arrived in the usual smoke blackened tin cans and was hastily enjoyed. It was taken as something of a loss of face for a man's machine to be standing while others were working. John wasn't going to have any time wasted on his.

The main shaft is 'drifted' out, using a 28-lb sledge-hammer. As I toiled away at it making small progress, suddenly I heard, "Give me dat ting."

Wonderingly, I handed John the hammer, and I held up in place the heavy steel dolly used to protect the machined shaft end from the hammer blows. I knew that if John missed I would probably have no hands left...

At the first blow, the machine visibly jerked, and as blow after blow struck with deadly accuracy, I could almost hear it asking for mercy. In next to no time, the shaft was driven out. With unspoken relief, I asked John where he had learned to 'use' a hammer.

"When I was fourteen, they took me on in *Harland and Wolf's* in Belfast as a striker (hammer man)," he said.

He had certainly lost none of his skill. The effective use of a heavy hammer is really as much skill as strength; it is also a marvellous body exercise.

* * *

On a couple of occasions, Glasgow cattle mart was stricken with the highly infectious foot and mouth disease. The standard procedure then was to immediately close the mart and slaughter all the animals within it. These had to be buried and this was done in ground attached to Dalmuir Sewage Works, which lay to the west of the city. Bulldozers were used to dig trenches for the purpose and afterwards cover them up again.

On a wet and dark Saturday night, I had just put my feet up when the telephone rang and I was summoned to help John Friary at Dalmuir, where he had just succeeded in stalling his bulldozer in the burial trench, and was unable to restart it.

It was only after I had done the necessary and we were tidying up that I realised that John wasn't entirely sober, and considering the conditions, I didn't really blame him. Thankfully, he decided that enough was enough and accepted a lift homewards across the city.

As we drove down Maryhill Road and were passing a large modern Roman Catholic chapel, from the tail of my eye I noticed John swiftly crossing himself and in the same instant, he started to rebuke me for not doing likewise. He quickly remembered that I was not of the RC persuasion, so, apologising, he continued, "Is it not terrible…me a fool like this and me brother a passionate father in Dublin."

Nevertheless, John was of cast iron material and a tremendous asset to have on any site.

* * *

Jack Dempsy was not a tall man. When I knew him, he was probably the wrong side of sixty. His working life started at the age of thirteen as second man (fireman) on a *Foden* steam lorry running between Glasgow and Aberdeen.

On a day of light snow and hard frost, he had been driving a large *Caterpillar (D8)* hauling an earth-moving 'scraper', pioneering an open cast coal site in Lanarkshire. As he travelled across a gradient, the outfit suddenly lost its footing and shot sideways downhill, coming to rest on its side in a frozen burn. Jack, quicker than it takes to tell, landed on his back on the ice, the machine rocking itself to a standstill above him. Shaken, but realising he was going to live he climbed to his feet.

Coming on site next day to salvage the machinery, I was interested to know all details. "What did you do then?" I asked.

"I bought a half bottle (of whisky) on my way home and drank it and went to my bed."

Salvage went smoothly and there was no damage to man or machine; end of story.

* * *

The three brothers McQuade were expert operators and a pleasure to have in the team. Willing and totally proficient, each could instantly adapt to any type of machine, crane, bulldozer, excavator – it made no difference to them.

Father Mcquade had been a public works general foreman. He had spent years travelling from one big job to another, probably mainly living on site. Consequently his sons, with the exception of the eldest, John, grew up with machinery as natural to them as motorcars are now. John used to complain that his younger brothers had an unfair advantage over him, being more or less weaned and reared in the back of excavators, whereas from the age of fourteen, he had been sent away to the Navy as a brat (boy apprentice).

One winter's day, on my routine rounds, I called on John, who was involved in the construction of a NATO refuelling depot at Loch Striven near Dunoon. John's countenance reminded me of a rock face somewhere on a severe climb and he was probably fifteen years my senior. He had come off his machine and was watching me with an unusual concern as I approached him on foot.

*Jack Dempsy's
stricken outfit*

"What did you come for Hector?"

Myself: "Oh, just to see how you're getting on, John."

John: "I'm glad of that. I thought you had come to chastise me, and if there's one thing I can't abide, it's being chastised."

This, after having been aboard HMS *Amethyst* which ran the gauntlet down the Yangtze river under fire from the Chinese communists – an incident which was high drama in the media of the time.

Not long back in the UK when the Dunkirk evacuation was imminent, John's Navy pal one day told of a 'great' discovery he had made. HMS *Gypsy* was almost ready for sea at Newcastle and the Navy was quietly recruiting volunteers to crew it for a special mission.

"It would be the greatest thing since sliced bread," and he persuaded John to join him as a volunteer.

In fact, the *Gypsy* had been hastily equipped as an anti-aircraft vessel for the great evacuation at Dunkirk. Early in the proceedings, it was sunk underneath them, and John and his friend were left on an inflated dingy somewhere off the French coast. A passing German aircraft added to their discomfort with a spray of machine gun fire that put several holes in the dingy. As the two of them frantically tore up their shirts to plug the holes, John relates that he addressed his 'friend' as follows: "If I ever get out of this, you b--------, I'll murder you..."

* * *

I cannot leave these great guys without reference to John (Darkie) McBride. John was a small dark Irishman, placid as a pond in summer, he could charm and placate the most irate G F (general foreman) with the greatest of ease. Like most of his buddies, he was a master at the controls of his bulldozer, but I will pass on to my last meeting with him.

Long after I had left the muck-shifting scene and was settled in Inverness, my brother-in-law rang me from East Kilbride and said, "Did you see who was on the front page of the *Daily Record* yesterday?"

Of course, I had not. Ian went on to tell me the article was about Darkie McBride, mugged and robbed on his way to the bank to deposit £1,500 for his funeral expenses, **aged 100**. It just happened that some time later I was in Glasgow on business, and being free in the afternoon, I went in search of Darkie.

I new roughly where he had lived some 40 years earlier and I homed in on the area. On a beautiful summer's day, as I drove slowly down a street, I noticed in my driving mirror, a man walking on the pavement in my direction; there was no one else around. I reversed to make contact. Reaching him, I enquired, "Have you ever heard of a man Darkie McBride in these parts?"

Immediate reply: "Last Close at the bottom of the street...two up on the right, Jock...shout through the letter box...he's pretty deaf. If he's not there, he'll be in the bookie's office across the street."

As I entered the bookie's office, there he was, Andy Cap bonnet and cigarette in mouth with a long curved ash hanging on the end of it. Darkie was concentrating on the tele screen high on the wall. As I approached him, he greeted me with, "Ach, I recognised you as soon as you came in."

After we exchanged pleasantries, I said, "That was a shame you loosing all that money, John."

"Ach," he said, "what would I want it for anyway...I make about twenty quid a day in here most days. Sure, I've been getting cards with money from all over. There was one with £50, another with £30, some with £20. I've got most of it back already, and besides that, one day the undertaker came in here and he said when the time comes he'll bury me for nothing anyway. Here, have a cigarette, Hector."

He was slightly puzzled that I didn't smoke cigarettes anymore.

Then he said, "You know, one day there was a couple of fellows from the IRA came in here to see me; they were from Dublin. One of them was me (my) late wife's brother-in-law and they had heard about me. They were asking me about these fellows. They say they're going to find them. They say they have their methods. I don't know what their methods are, but they say they're going to find them."

Personally, I can only say I'm glad I'm not one of these fellows. We reminisced some on the old days, but eventually reluctantly I had to take my leave.

* * *

The health and safety arrangements of the era left a lot to be desired. Willie Bennie and his machine were working at the tunnel face inside Ben Cruachan in Argyllshire where a large pumped storage hydroelectric generating station was under construction. The tunnel tigers, in their usual bonus-inspired enthusiasm, had overdone it with their explosives, damaging our machine and wrecking the tunnel lighting system. As it often was for such occasions, it was evening, and the plant engineer required my company to assess the damage or effect repairs. With our best guess at the necessary tools and equipment aboard, we sped up the seventy miles to the north shore of Lochawe and the Cruachan works base. A contractor's man advised us that there would be a dumper going into the tunnel to the work face in ten minutes and we could get in with it. And so we boarded, one each side clinging onto the skip of a small builders-type dumper. Apart from a swivelling rear axle, these machines have no form of suspension whatsoever. Its load, the most incongruous imaginable – a few cartons of electric light bulbs and precariously above them, heavy steel oxygen and acetylene cylinders, bouncing unrestrained as we rattled and bounced on the rough tunnel floor. The remaining tunnel lighting was absolutely minimal and the dumper had none.

Some minutes later, we discovered that the tunnel spoil was being extracted using 'giant' *Eimco* articulated dump trucks. Their relative size to our transport would be something of the order of a steam loco and a mini car. Even above the 'bang, bang, bang…' of our single-cylinder engine, we heard the roar of one approaching. To say the least, the dumper passengers began to feel some concern, as we saw the faint glimmer of the approaching monster's one defective headlight come into view. Suddenly, our dumper driver slackened off and veered to a halt in a slight recess in the tunnel wall. He reached into his breast pocket, fumbled and found a cigarette lighter which he lit and slowly waved to and fro, hopefully to be seen by the driver of the monster thundering towards us – and then it was past. Little wonder some fourteen men lost their lives on that contract!

Chapter 11

High Places

I began to feel the need for a change of scene. A former school
pal of mine, Martin Hill, a civil engineer, had reached a
position of some power in the southern branch of a north
contractor, *Duncan Logan (Contractors) Ltd.* I contacted him to
ask if he would act as referee for me in relation to a position I had
applied for with the South of Scotland Electricity Board. His
immediate response was, "Why don't you come and work with
us?"

Thus I became plant inspector in Logan's, based at Muirhead
just out of Glasgow on the Stirling road.

The company's roots were in a small builder's business based in
Muir of Ord, and under the leadership of the late Willie Logan,
son of the founder, it had mushroomed into a major construction
company, winning large contracts against the biggest in the land.

Willie Logan's confidence and vision seemed to know no
bounds. Sadly, his life ended prematurely in an air crash on the
wooded hill above Bunchrew. Willie had had the great gift of
being able to size up even the biggest contracts on the virgin
ground and arrive at a price in his head. When afterwards, his
engineers got down to their more professional procedure of
measuring, pricing, etc., they usually found Willie's price to be
within striking distance.

Though without professional training, he was technically
brilliant. Time and again he would come up with simple solutions
to difficult engineering problems without recourse to calculations.

When I joined, *Logan's* were on the crest of the contracting
wave, with millions of pounds of work in hand, not least of which
was the construction of the 1¾ miles road bridge linking Dundee
with Fife across the Tay estuary.

I quickly had to familiarise myself with a new lot of colleagues, workshop staff and machine operators for whom I was made responsible, and all manner of plant and machinery which included small railway locomotives, tower cranes, 100-ton rail-mounted cranes, and the necessary for the construction of a 300-foot high factory chimney. I even found myself locating and buying an old locomotive for £400. It turned out to be a good one and it gave good service in the construction of the Tay Road Bridge.

The construction of the bridge was a 'hairy' kind of business. The bridge started from normal ground level at the Dundee end, rising to some 80 ft above the water at the Fife end.

I'd better not go into too much technical detail. Suffice it to say that the finished article stands on concrete columns topped by 200-ton steel box beams, which had to be hoisted into place from not much above high water level. Constructed on shore, the beams were rolled out to their location on a temporary rail bridge that had two standard gauge rail tracks side by side. These rail tracks provided the travel path for the cranes used for all material handling.

I was fascinated by the cranes, which were standard crawler cranes mounted on rail undercarriages – custom built to Willie's design. They spanned and sat on the double rail line. The all-up weight of a crane unit was 110 tons, each with sixteen wheels on the rails. The heavy cranes had a wooden walkway running along their cab sides. I was intrigued one day at the homely sight of a crane operator sitting on a box on his walkway, peeling spuds for his midday meal, no doubt also catering for a few of his pals. All meals on the bridge were taken, literally, on the job.

While the main temporary bridge had timber decking and safety rails, a further temporary single-track rail bridge tacked on, on the upstream side, had neither. It was on this bridge the eight-ton locomotives ran, hauling wagons with concrete, steel, timber and all the paraphernalia associated with a major contract.

In my early visits to Dundee, access to plant on the bridge was simple – walking out on the wooden decking of the main temporary bridge – but as progress was made, hazards started to appear. Each concrete pillar was built in a watertight cofferdam founded on the bedrock below the river. Several pillars were being built simultaneously, early ones being bypassed and the temporary bridging giving way to a single steel beam eight or ten inches wide spanning each cofferdam. Some of the beams had a rickety safety rail on one side only, while others had none.

Not having a head for heights, I found it quite sobering, walking out over the beams high above an excavator and squad of men working below, and at the same time trying hard to appear unconcerned.

The Tay estuary always had a fierce current flowing either upstream or downstream depending on whether the tide was flooding or ebbing.

Sadly, there were a number of fatalities   during the contract. There was a row of permanently manned rescue boats straining at their rope tethers, one side of the bridge or the other. The most successful of these had a shrewd Hebridean boatman, who when the call came, instead of starting his engine, simply cast off and, carried by the current, seldom failed to effect a rescue of the 'man overboard'.

One very stormy day when the job was well advanced, I found, as I made my way to inspect machinery, that the route took me up a series of ladders and onto the top of the main bridge beams high above the river. The beams were about ten feet wide with no guard-rails. Ten feet may sound a very adequate width to walk on, but with a gale strength wind suddenly gusting and subsiding, it was a different matter. To stay on course in a gust, I had to lean heavily into the wind, and as a gust suddenly subsided, rapid straightening up was necessary to prevent myself going over the side.

Sometimes, reluctantly, I availed myself of a lift on a loco heading out on the bridge. I say 'reluctantly' because the nature of the loco bridge and track was in the famous words of Para Handy such as to make one 'pause and consider'. The bridge was flimsy looking, but no doubt of adequate steel construction, topped with two slender looking rail lines and no decking.

Probably due to settlement and other reasons, it was no longer straight and level, but weaved very noticeably, in both horizontal and vertical planes. In addition, where one rail met another, many had a distinct step up or down. The unsprung locos passed over these steps with shudders and loud bangs. A derailment most likely would mean a tumble into the Tay. *Logan's* canny general foreman described the loco driving as not being a job for lassies, (one driver at least was drowned when his loco tumbled off the bridge).

In spite of today's fixation on equal opportunities, I don't think there would be many takers from the female gender.

* * *

At *Logan's* southern HQ at Muirhead, I shared a large office with three others, one of whom was the late George (better known as 'Geordie') Ross from Maryburgh, near Dingwall. Geordie had been Willie Logan's star low-loader driver. A warm hearted modest man of short stature, he was accustomed to hauling loads in excess of fifty tons over single track west coast roads. His trailer was built in the Muir of Ord engineering workshop, again to Willie's design. There would have been no drawing to work to. Willie would simply have gone with a sketch, to his genius engineering shop manager, Andrew Gammie, and say, "Andrew, I need a trailer to carry so and so," to which Andrew would reply, "Ay, ay"…and just get on with it.

With the firm's move into the south of Scotland, it became necessary to have a transport manager, and Geordie was reluctantly moved from his low-loader to a desk in an office. With the clanishness of the Highlander, he warmly welcomed my arrival on the scene.

The firm won a new contract just west of Renfrew. The job called for several heavy crawler cranes. As Geordie planned the

135

transport, a big obstacle turned up in the form of an old road over a rail bridge with a fifteen-ton weight restriction. There appeared to be no other way into the site. I suggested that the old Renfrew vehicle ferry might solve the problem.

The ferry, now long since gone, took the form of what looked like a huge steel shoe box with open ends. Vehicles would drive aboard at one riverbank and off at the other. It hauled itself back and forth across the Clyde on two heavy steel chains, anchored at each riverbank and normally lying on the riverbed to allow the passage of shipping.

Geordie invited me for an exploratory trip. On arrival, we had to wait the 'shoebox's' arrival from the far side. There was one crewman on deck shepherding the traffic. There followed a brief conversation...

Geordie: "What's your maximum vehicle weight?"

Crewman: "Fifteen tons."

Geordie groaned and turned away.

Crewman: "What weight have you got?"

Geordie: "About thirty five tons."

Crewman: "Nae bother, bring it down."

Geordie: "Are you sure? How much will it cost?"

Crewman: "Och aye, nae problem, it'll be three and six. (Three shillings and sixpence – in current values, seventeen and a half pence).

* * *

Every weekend for nine years that I know of, Geordie and one or two of his cronies motored north on the A9, home for the weekend, a journey of about 170 miles, arriving back at work around nine o'clock each Monday morning. Apart from one occasion when the snowdrifts beat him at Dalwhinnie, he never failed to complete his journey. In those days, the snow gates on the road were closed when necessary, but not padlocked. When they were closed, Geordie opened them, drove through and closed them behind him. On the occasion when he got stuck, Willie

Logan sensing the need, mustered a couple of helpers and successfully rescued him with his *Rolls Royce.*

* * *

One of the most ferocious battles of the Second World War was the battle of the Anzio beachhead in Italy. Geordie had been a tank driver but I only heard him once make reference to his wartime experiences. I don't know how the subject came up, but he spoke because of his admiration for one man. He told me how he had been sitting in his tank lined up with the rest of his squadron at Anzio, waiting for the signal to move in a strong attack on the German positions. There was ammunition flying everywhere and there was the Unit Chaplain walking from one tank to the next, having a word with the crews 'while we sat inside, shaking with bravery'.

My office desk sat front to front with that of another colleague, Percy Walker, one of the shrewdest characters I've ever come across. I once heard him described as the ultimate in craftiness – the man who could pee in a fox's ear without wakening it.

In the 1960s, it was boom time in Britain and there were a number of people setting up in business as 'Efficiency Consultants to Industry' and making a nice living out of it. Such was the suave gent shown in to call on Percy one day.

Percy had noticed the arrival of a shining *Bentley* car through the office window. The visitor introduced himself and the nature of his business, but before he could get any further, Percy said, "Is that your car out there?"

Smiling with pleasure in anticipation of Percy's admiration, the poor man said it was indeed.

"Well," said Percy, "how can anybody that knows anything about efficiency run the most inefficient car on the road? I think you better leave now. Goodbye, Mr X."

I must mention Rab Dempster, a bulldozer driver, a gracious man who was totally deaf.

Rab had been given a new *Euclid* machine to operate, probably the first of its type in Scotland. Not many days had passed till he reported a 'knock' in the engine. Manufacturer's engineers were summoned, did their thing and said there was no fault... everything was OK. Nevertheless, two days later, a con-rod came through the side of the crankcase, totally wrecking the engine.

* * *

A situation arose which nobody I knew had ever encountered before. Because of urgency and chronic abuse on a motorway contract, a vital heavy *Ruston Bucyrus* excavator had literally bent its back to the extent that its main driving gears had separated, so that they had come right out of mesh. The teeth could no longer reach each other. It was a serious situation; there was no replacement machine available. Progress on the whole contract was drastically affected.

There is an aspect to public works that the general public tend to be largely unaware of. Apart from wartime, there is usually fierce competition for contracts among contractors. Normally, the cheapest price will win the job. Consequently, prices are pared to the bone and very often further, in the hope that the usually inevitable 'extras' will result in a profit being made. Every additional day in the use of men and machines soaks up money, minimising the prospects of a profit.

News of our latest crises had broken in mid-afternoon. Normally in our plant office when any special difficulty arose, heads went together till the matter was resolved. This time on the point of five o'clock, Percy purposefully lifted his brief case and headed for home. Pausing at the door on his way, he turned and said, "There's just one thing to do, Hector lad."

My spirits rose, expecting some wonderful solution to my problem, and as quickly subsided as the next words were delivered – "Go at it bold, lad! Goodnight."

By the grace of God, before I left that night I managed to contact a *Ruston* works engineer who was on a courtesy visit to Glasgow. He promised to come and have a look next morning.

I still marvel at his skill. Defying convention, he came up with a near certain solution. He quickly took the necessary dimensions, designed a larger replacement gear wheel to bridge the gap, faxed the drawing to his works and had them manufacture it as an emergency. The latter was no mean feat in itself, as *Ruston Bucyrus* were not much given to emergencies, preferring standard hours and practises. Nevertheless the outcome was totally successful.

* * *

Logan's Muirhead base covered a large area with open country on three sides. One day coming out of the office and heading for the workshop, I heard the most blood curdling squeals and screeches, but couldn't see their source till I came in sight of the road below the bank I was on. There below me, a weasel had a large rat by the throat. The rat, much the heavier of the two was on its back screeching the screeches of terror, and frantically throwing itself from one side to the other, flinging the weasel from side to side trying vainly to shake it off, but all to no purpose. I stood stock still, just about mesmerised myself. Finally, the noise stopped and the tiny victor trailed his prize away out of sight into the long grass.

* * *

Some of the Muirhead workshop staff were not of the standard I would like to have. A shining exception was an apprentice fitter, Willie. Willie, a tall fair-haired lad, first appeared at my office accompanied by his father who did all the talking. Father turned out to be a cattleman in local employment. No frills with father. He wore just his normal dungaree jacket and trousers topped off with a bonnet. As soon as Willie turned sixteen and was thus able to leave school, father brought him along to seek an apprenticeship for him. I was impressed with both, and the following Monday, Willie started his career.

Somewhat to our surprise, he was totally polite and respectful, always addressing both his foreman and myself as 'sir'. He

139

learned rapidly and as soon as he became seventeen, passed his driving test. The foreman fitter, Jock Macpherson from Beauly, grew so confident in Willie that he started sending him to attend to breakdowns on site, a function for which older, more experienced men would normally be used.

Willie had just returned from such a job some 30 or 40 miles away, when he apologised to Jock for having to spend a small sum of money to buy some essential material that he did not have with him, and 'Could he please have the money refunded?'

Jock being much more accustomed to men who in such a situation would return and report failure on account of the material shortage, was delighted with such initiative from an apprentice and told him he would add some extra hours to his time sheet as a reward. Willie wouldn't hear of it. He said emphatically, "No, sir."

"But why?" said Jock.

Willie: "Because my *faither* would kill me."

Enough said.

* * *

I've already said that I had lost my head for heights. One day the managing director Martin Hill sent for me and launched into the subject of tower cranes. He told me how the company's tower cranes had been bought from a French company. He explained that from time to time crane tower heights had to be increased until on completion of its work, the whole machine had to be dismantled. Up till that time, the supplier's men had been called in to do the work and in his opinion they were taking *Logan's* 'to the cleaners'. Therefore, would I go away and put together our own team, if possible from within the company, and from any site where I found suitable people.

Slightly shocked and not daring to tell him about my height problem, I took my leave. Like the loco driving on the Tay bridge, tower crane erecting and dismantling, (in all weathers – with one exception) is definitely 'not a job for lassies'. The one weather exception is 'wind speed'.

The crane manual clearly states that the work must only be done in conditions of no wind. In Scotland, such a condition occurred at ground level all right, but in my experience never above a height of fifty feet.

I felt strongly that I couldn't ask men to do what I was not prepared to do myself. In the actual work, from a safety point of view, on account of the constant moving about necessary on the structure, it isn't really practical to use safety harnesses.

* * *

I've already mentioned my growing interest in the Bible and now I was attending each Sunday at Drumchapel Free Church of Scotland. I started going there because of an invitation from a good friend, Alaister Macrae from Ullapool. Happily, Willie Logan was a lifelong Free Church man and in accordance with the fourth Commandment, except in exceptional circumstances, none of his men worked on Sundays.

For the first time in my life, I was paid by monthly salary, and the arrangement suited me very well. I was able to attend church most Sundays. It was a standard ruling in construction work that all Sunday work be paid for at double pay rate. Therefore, with a big mortgage, my new conditions suited me.

* * *

One Sunday I was in church, my crane height problem was still gnawing away at me, and the minister, Hector Cameron, in his sermon quoted the words of Jesus, 'And whatsoever ye shall ask in my name, that will I do' and it appeared that he was looking straight at me. The words certainly registered deep within me.

Although I was speaking to Rebecca whilst driving home, the miracle that is the human mind was marvelling that the words of Jesus exactly matched my needs for the crane situation, and I silently resolved to put them to the test.

In later life, I quail at my presumption – not in ascending a tower crane, but in 'testing' the word of God.

I came across another quote from Jesus 'All things whatsoever you shall ask in prayer, <u>believing</u>, you shall receive'.

The next Saturday afternoon, I drove to the site at Cumbernauld Town Centre building. I knew that it was unlikely that anyone would be about. Having prayed to God in Jesus' name, I made my way to the nearest tower crane, scrambled inside its tower where the steel-runged ladder is and started my climb.

I suppose that to many people, a hundred and something feet up a ladder may not seem any great task, but as a forty-year-old, now largely office-bound, I found myself starting to blow a bit. I was glad to reach the first of several tiny rest platforms on the way up – there to pause, recover my breath and review my position. I emerged onto the little railed platform surrounding the driver's cabin at the top. Everything above that level, cabin included, could swing full circle as the crane went about its business.

The erecting and maintenance of a crane can entail work at the extreme end of its jib, in this case, 120 feet long. Access to it is by walking carefully along the three-inch wide bottom runner, which forms the bottom angle of the triangular section jib. One can keep a hand on the fat tubular apex runner, but otherwise it is total exposure to the ground somewhere below. I had, of course, to prove completely the exercise I was engaged on. The jib was still a good ten feet above me. How to get to it? Up a short ladder into the cab, push open the roof trapdoor up the ladder behind the operator's seat, and onto the cabin roof.

There, safe and surrounded by the narrowing steelwork of the tower top, again in Para Handy's famous words, I was able to 'pause and consider'. As I looked out along the jib, its length appeared to have at least doubled. With shortened breath, I prayed earnestly for safe conduct, and squeezed out from my 'crow's nest' onto the jib. With great caution I set off for the other end, pausing frequently to give the impression to any observer that I was simply weighing up the machinery and the site in general.

With maximum concentration, I reached my destination and was thankful to find a little rest platform of steel mesh. Round its outer edge there was a 'safety' rail at about one foot above the platform. Here I felt it wise to sit down and pray for safe return, which was happily granted.

From there on, tower crane work went smoothly. My adventure on the crane jib was proof to me, if I needed any, that there is a God, that God is; in the Bible, He simply says 'I am'.

I quickly found three willing lads for the little crane team. One of them, Jimmie Steel, in addition to his name, appeared also to have nerves of steel. He would happily stand on the three-inch runner, reach in his pocket chat and proffer a cigarette.

One day, we were putting up a crane at Dunbar cement works. I happened to be talking to the site general foreman (no 'lassie' himself) when there was a call from aloft: "Hector, where does this go'?"

There was Jimmie standing on the 'three inches' and holding up a large steel component. I answered the question, and the foreman said to me, "Is he mad?" I assured him Jimmie was of sound mind.

* * *

An ironic situation arose one day while we were working. A fairly new crane operator slipped, fell almost through the jib, and was saved only by steel struts of the jib catching under his armpits. Quick as a flash, very strong Jimmie grabbed him by his jacket shoulders and hoisted him to safety. The fellow was naturally and visibly shaken, so Jimmie applied his treatment for shock. His arm round him to keep him from falling, with his free hand he managed to find a cigarette, lit it and thrust into the man's mouth with the instruction 'pull on that' – producing unexpected results. There was extensive coughing, spluttering and reddening of cheeks before the faint words came, "I don't smoke, Jock."

* * *

From fear of heights, I graduated to working at nearly 300 feet. Again at Dunbar cement works, *Logan's* were building a 300-foot high chimney of concrete, cast *in situ*. They were getting near 'top-out' when a factory inspector came on site and condemned the steel ropes on the hoist that was being used, thus bringing the contract to a standstill – bad news!

It was early afternoon when I received the call, "What can you do, Hector?"

A quick think, probably a quick prayer, order and collect reels of new steel cable and with three good men at around 6 PM we set off on the 70-odd miles to Dunbar. We were blessed with a lovely evening and, on site, they had left us a willing and able ex-farm hand to help.

The Dunbar chimney stood 30 feet diameter at its base and tapered upwards, our hoist standing inside it. It had four separate and independent ropes, each of which was capable of taking the maximum load on its own. Each rope end was anchored at the tower top, the rope then passing over a system of pulleys and ending on the winding drum at the base, each rope having a total length of over a thousand feet.

I had never seen the pulley wheels, etc. at the top of the hoist tower and it seemed to me that here was my opportunity. Furthermore, since we had a pair of walkie-talkie radios, it seemed a good location from which to conduct operations. Ideally, we would have used the hoist cage to haul the first rope end up to its anchor at the top, but since the inspector had applied a prohibition notice on the use of the hoist, the only way to the top was by scrambling up the tower steelwork. Believe me, I was glad of a perched, but sitting, rest when I reached the top.

A few words on the radio and Jock Macpherson had despatched the farm man to the top with the first rope end. Whatever gifts he might have, he was certainly blessed with 'stickability' (stamina). The higher he went, the more weight of rope he was hauling with him. He reached the top, his tongue hanging out and quite speech-less. Once that rope was secured and reeved up, we were able to use the hoist cage for the remaining heavy work. Mercifully, it had been a calm moonlit night and, with the tower top protruding some ten to fifteen feet above the chimney top, I really had a bird's eye view of things below.

Throughout the night there were no rest breaks or cups of tea, but we had total success. Therefore, it was, to say the least, disappointing to be pulled over by a police car in Mussleburgh on our way home at around six in the morning, a few 'knots' over the speed limit. Fortunately, the policeman hailed from Plockton, and in good will from one 'hieland' man to another, he soon sent us on our way with something like, "Don't do it down here."

* * *

Out of the blue one Saturday morning came the shocking news that Willie Logan was dead. There had been heavy fog around Inverness and the chartered light plane in which he had travelled north for the weekend, had flown straight into the pine trees above Bunchrew. The fuselage had passed between two pine trees, slicing off both wings, and killing Willie instantly. The pilot, although badly injured, survived.

The company directors unanimously voted Martin Hill to take over the reins. This he did vigorously, winning many contracts, including, in a joint venture with an English contractor, the building of Glasgow's Kingston Bridge.

Martin was a dedicated worker. One afternoon he called me in to talk about a job the firm had been offered in Church St., Inverness – the erection of a large concrete structured building, the contract to be completed in one year. It was not to be turned down; there was no tendering of prices and therefore no competition. My interest in it would be the feasibility of erection and later dismantling of a tower crane in the very confined location. He reached a decision. "We'll just have to go up and see it. Meet me at the airport (Glasgow) at five o'clock."

A *Loganair* plane was waiting us and, job done, I was back home before 10 p.m.

* * *

Alas, all Martin's efforts were to no avail, the inevitable came and the company went into liquidation. In the north, most people laid the blame at Martin Hill's feet. "If Willie'd still been alive, it wouldn't have happened."

But had they known the full facts, I think they might have had a different opinion. My belief is that Willie had received a timely rescue. With a massive overdraft, among the disposable assets were two Rolls Royce cars and a third on order. Martin had been left with a rather sick baby to try to nurse back to health.

There were immediate redundancies; Martin Hill was among the first, and masses of materials and machinery were to be disposed of. There were 10,000 tons of steel sections and tubes salvaged from the temporary bridge at the Tay, lying at Dundee. The lot had to be hauled by company transport to the Muirhead yard to be sold off in lots at huge auction sales. Geordie Ross had a special trailer of 50 tons capacity built in our own workshop.

I was approached by the liquidator to stay on for a year at salary plus a third, probably the most lucrative period of my life.

As the months ran by, serious thought had to be given to future employment. New executive houses were advertised to rent in the new town of East Kilbride. Uncertain of how the cookie might crumble, it seemed a good idea to rent one and sell up in Bearsden. Thus we arrived in East Kilbride, complete with Snookie, the family cat, who within a couple of hours came in bearing a dead mouse and proudly presented it to Rebecca. At night we could hear owls hooting and a fox barking. Happily our house was not far from Rebecca's brother Ian, Christine his wife and their family.

Kenny pleased with a live furry friend at Dunblane
Highland Games

Chapter 12

And Low Places.

N ear the end of my time with the *Logan* liquidator, I saw an ad for a plant workshop manager with *Lilley Contractors*, a highly successful company in Govan district. They were family-owned, specialising in tunnelling and harbour works, and were one of the biggest contractors in Scotland, successfully winning contracts in England against strong opposition. Following a stiff interview before several directors and the company secretary, somewhat to my surprise, I got the job, along with a good salary and perks.

Company growth had been rapid and their machinery maintenance had been left behind. I found a yard full of unusable plant and a plant workshop geared to the pace of ten years previously. The plant holding was large and varied, including some 40 cranes, and, a complete novelty to me, tunnelling shields. These huge steel tubes gave protection to men as they dug their way into a tunnel face, pushing forward with a circle of large hydraulic rams. The shields conveniently broke down into sections for lowering and raising through a small diameter shaft, then to be built or dismantled underground. Not only did *Lilley* use them, but they had also bought over the company that manufactured them in the London area.

Shields moved forward by the rams pushing against concrete tunnel lining segments placed and secured behind them as they progressed. A curiosity of the system was that the shields imperceptibly rotated as they moved forward, and in spite of having steel stabilising fins like a submarine, they invariably finished the job topside down.

By employee opinion, the Lilleys were millionaires. Father paid an occasional visit to the depot, arriving in a chauffeur-driven

Rolls Royce. His two sons were in the business; the younger was my boss.

One day in his office, I excused myself to visit the loo. He expressed surprise, telling me that he 'got all that over with before he left home in the morning'. I refrained from pointing out to him that he didn't come to work till 10.00 AM.

* * *

It was quickly evident that the workshop needed a young and 'urgent' foreman. He came in the form of David Wilson, a trained locomotive engineer, young and clean living, but he had no experience of construction machinery. With considerable misgivings, I started him and it turned out to be one of my best decisions in *Lilley*. He was of strong character, polite, but standing no nonsense. To the surprise of my superiors, the yard was soon cleared of unusable plant. David exercised excellent diplomacy towards the existing foreman, Willie Kilfedder, who soon accepted the younger man.

Willie, a unique genius, now in his latter years, could literally fix anything that came his way – from large piling frames to wristwatches. When Brian Lilley's expensive watch was due servicing, it went to Willie, who dealt with it in his cubby-hole under the stair. I visited him a few years after his retirement and saw some beautiful grandfather and smaller clocks he had made, including the mechanism and woodwork – works of art.

Another huge asset who came our way was Donnie Murdoch from Achterneed near Strathpeffer. Donnie was a meticulous and expert engine man. His hobby was motorcycle racing. He had his own *Suzuki* racing bike, which he transported in his van at the weekends to many of the English race meetings. He often got a place, usually third or second. He told me he couldn't afford to go for a first. That usually went to wealthy entrants with one or two back up mounts, and it didn't matter to them if they crashed a bike.

One Monday I noticed Donnie limping badly. I asked him what the trouble was. "Oh, I came off the bike yesterday."

Myself: "What speed were you doing?"

Donnie: "About eighty," as if it was an everyday occurrence.

Between each use, the bike engine was completely dismantled and every part lovingly polished and perhaps a little bit shaved off here and there to gain absolute maximum performance.

Rebecca started looking about for a house to buy and found it in No.6, Station Road, Bardowie, a hamlet just north of Glasgow. Bardowie consisted of a scattering of houses along a main road and a further handful on Station Road, wide and unpaved, twenty minutes from the city centre by car. For us, it had a lot going for it; at heart we were really country people, and this had it all. Bardowie didn't even have street lighting, open country around us, sounds of wild life at night, and within comfortable walking distance of the *River Kelvin*. It was here that Seoras caught his first fish, a pike, and very pleased he was with his capture.

The races *in our Bardowie garden*

Just across the main road was the picturesque Bardowie Loch. Best of all, for the first time in our lives we were able to buy without a mortgage. Although we had Station Road, we had no station, the new town which it had been intended to serve, had never been built and although there were level crossing gates down by the *Kelvin*, the railway lines had gone in the Dr. Beeching cuts. We had Baldernock Parish Church, still with a little stone outbuilding, shelter for those who in times past had to guard against body snatchers. The church had a little bonus attraction for our boys, in the form of the chain which hung down the outside of the building, and still used as in days past for ringing the bell to announce the time of morning worship.

The chain was operated by Bert the butcher, who was generous in giving little boys a shot of ringing the bell.

Baldernock Parish Church

Bardowie was a golden period in our lives. Rebecca became a member of the WRI (Women's Rural Institute) in the neighbouring

151

village, Torrance. She enjoyed going there on her bicycle; probably to keep her hair in order, she wore a black tammy on the way. It was a time of intense Irish troubles; there were often scenes on the telly showing IRA men with rifles and black tammies. One evening just after Rebecca's departure, complete with black tammy, Kenny, four years old, earnestly asked, "Dad, why does Mam go to the IRA?"

* * *

The *Lilley* firm's good fortune continued. The planners had routed a new section of ring road through their yard; I understand adequate compensation was forthcoming for a new large yard and purpose-built buildings in the Springburn area of the city. A massive exercise was mounted to move everybody and everything over a weekend between stopping time on Friday evening and normal service resuming at 8 a.m. Monday. I fell heir to a fine office with an outlook over the city and to the hills beyond. That was in 1971 – now, thirty-three years later, the ring road has still not been built!

* * *

All good things come to an end, or so the world says. I personally believe that if the hand of God is on you, he has a good reason for every setback He allows you to experience. On a bright and sunny day, our Contracts Director had been showing the Glasgow city engineer over an important contract on Union Street right in the city centre. It involved a large excavation and temporary sewer diversion, which in turn required over-pumping of the sewage flow past the excavation.

A replacement pump from our workshop had just been set to work. A careless workshop fitter had failed to properly tighten four vital bolts, and just as the important visitor was passing, the bolts had worked loose sufficiently to cause the pump to start discharging its output of raw sewage straight onto Union Street. My first knowledge of the happening was when I was called to the workshop telephone.

The caller was the Contracts Director, and to say he was livid would be an understatement; he was all but melting the phone wires. I still hadn't been able to say a word when to add fuel to the fire, we were suddenly cut off, and I suspect he may have thought I had hung up on him. About a quarter of an hour later, I was speaking with someone in my own office when the door suddenly burst open; in he came and started again from where he had left off.

Eventually he ran out of steam, and still glowing, he left.

While I can well understand his embarrassment and even more his deeply wounded pride, in nearly three years of a copious output of overhauled plant, including scores of pumps from our workshop, it was the first ever failure of a single item. I still didn't know in detail what had actually happened, and in hindsight, I have to confess that more than his pride had been wounded. I had given far beyond the standard 'pound of flesh' at *Lilley* and was generally heavily over-stretched; I was aggrieved at my treatment, my nose was out of joint, but such is the power and clout of a Contracts Director within a large construction company that men often regard them as nearly divine. Regrettably, in my experience, there the resemblance ended. I decided that enough was enough.

I made Rebecca aware of the situation. I then saw an ad in the paper for a plant manager in the Fort William area. I applied, was interviewed, and got the job. While working my notice in Glasgow, people warned me in very unfavourable terms of the kind of man I was going to work for, but nothing daunted, and despite requests from our Plant Director to change my mind, I pressed on.

Thereafter, for a short time, each weekend I motored home from Fort William to Glasgow.

The Bardowie house sold easily, but we soon discovered that in our new area, houses were much pricier, in fact beyond our reach without a mortgage, and we did not want to be encumbered with one again.

Chapter 13

Some Changes

*M*y new boss volunteered to make a large residential caravan available for us, but I soon had cause to remember the warnings I had been given in Glasgow. Our small boys were far from happy at their new school and Rebecca didn't seem all that happy. While many people are obliged to raise their family in a caravan, we did not want to do so.

There was a distinct incompatibility at work. At the time, violent explosions were the order of the day in the Irish 'troubles'. There was a small contract running at Lochaline on the west coast, and a company explosives magazine there was in the charge of a self-employed Irishman. Irish fishing boats made calls at Lochaline. Probably because I had a friend in the CID and MI6 who was quite involved in the Irish scene, I was more aware than most of the potential.

My confidence was not improved when one day I decided to give our plant store the once-over. In the dirty and untidy building, I found in old wooden drawers, sticks of gelignite and detonators mixed at random with tools, etc., that had seen better days. This was a dangerous and illegal practice. Explosives and detonators must only be stored in a steel magazine, manufactured to strict specifications and always in separate compartments. The store man considered the situation quite normal.

Suddenly, crises came. Throughout my life I had been fairly resilient, but now I started cracking up. Every morning, I left for work with tears streaming down my face. Little things grew out of all proportion. I hated every moment at work and in the area. Nearby Ben Nevis seemed the place to end it all, but my heart was torn for the family, especially our two little boys – so vulnerable.

On a Saturday, we took a trip to Inverness and house-hunted. There appeared to be only two on the market suitable to our needs and price. A semi-detached at 6 Pict Avenue seemed to be the one for us. It had obviously been empty for some time. We were able to peer in the windows and the grass in the back garden was knee high. Nevertheless, what we could see was fully carpeted; it seemed a quiet area, and it had a nearby modern primary school. Rebecca efficiently attended to the formalities for purchase. Again, although now almost penniless, we had a home and no mortgage.

On the day we received the keys, a nasty incident occurred. We had looked over the interior and were about to leave for Fort William when a loose concrete coping 'stone' from the garden wall fell and landed on five-year-old Kenny's toes. I was in anguish for him as we bundled him into the car and rushed to Raigmore hospital. His squashed big toe has largely recovered but still bears the evidence.

It didn't seem a good omen for a future in Inverness, but I knew Inverness was on the up and up and close to plenty oil-related work. I also knew that Jock Macpherson, previously of *Logans*, was now working with *Tulloch's*, another family-owned firm based in nearby Nairn. They were heavily involved in the development of a steel fabrication yard for North Sea oil.

Tulloch's interests included earth moving, civil engineering, building, timber and even funeral undertaking. I rang Jock; he thought my prospects were good and asked me to ring him back in a couple of days.

The result was, if I was willing to work with my tools again, to start as soon as I could and there would be a company van available.

* * *

Thus started a new phase of our lives, albeit on 50% less earnings than we had been accustomed to. Somehow we struggled by, Rebecca's economic skills and good cheer playing a big part.

For years I had always enjoyed a good but cold breakfast – cornflakes, a sprinkling of muesli with a liberal scattering of raisins on top and some sort of fresh fruit chopped up on top of that. Now I gave up the muesli and fruit and strictly counted the raisins, allowing myself ten for each meal.

Prior to my 'crack up', my Fort William employer had bought over my very nice car, thus there was now no family transport. Nevertheless, with plenty hard work, long hours and tight finances, my years in *Tulloch's* were happy ones; my colleagues were mainly 'couthy' country types.

After a while, I was able to buy a chain-saw with which I was able to augment fuel supplies for our solid fuel fire with birch blocks and others from here and there. After a couple of years, I was given a new *Toyota* van, which was an excellent vehicle. As is usual in our industry, everywhere I went, it was in a hurry and thereby hangs another tale.

* * *

There was a bulldozer working at Fort William. There were cold snaps of frost threatening and late one afternoon I was sent, probably overloaded, with several large containers of antifreeze mix for it. The A96 road – Nairn to Inverness – at that time sported a level crossing at Gollanfield. I had just crossed it and was belting towards the incline ahead, a solid stream of traffic coming the other way, when suddenly there appeared over the brow of the hill, a vehicle, overtaking at speed and coming towards me – right in my path. The situation would most likely have been fatal for both parties, but: -

I thank God for my reflexes, which responded instantly. Before I knew it the *Toyota* was hammering along on the grass border beside the road, the offending vehicle now out of sight in the opposite direction. I steered to regain the roadway, but the inertia of my liquid load took over and the *Toyota* proceeded diagonally right across my lane and the one with the oncoming traffic. To brake would have been suicide as I cut across the bows of a loaded tipper truck. Ahead was a gentle grass rise to a field fence, and as van met fence, it straightened up astride the fence still at a fair pace and felled twenty fence posts in a row.

I know, because next day I went back and counted them.

Highly embarrassed, I got out to review my situation. The off-side front hub cap was lying on the grass; I took it and pushed it back in place. Otherwise, the van appeared to be undamaged because the fence posts were rotten.

You may say, "Why didn't you brake then?"

I don't know, maybe I did; everything happened so fast – I cannot tell. I do know that, just then my swishing liquid load was causing the van to veer back towards the road and the oncoming heavy traffic, it was as if an invisible hand took hold, and the van came to a smooth and immediate stop, almost touching a large gorse bush in front.

But why had it stopped so conveniently?

Looking underneath, I saw the reason – a single strand of fence wire hooked between the rear spring leaves. It had acted just as an arrester wire would on an aircraft carrier – coincidence or the hand of God? I prefer to believe the latter. A driver from a passing lorry had stopped to help and with a push from him, I managed to regain the road through a gap in the traffic. Without further ado, I headed for Fort William and completed my mission, returning home to a good meal and rest.

* * *

Tulloch's heavy earthmovers were largely employed in shifting vast quantities of sand on the oil site near Ardersier. Sand, by virtue of its abrasive nature, wears out tracks at a phenomenal rate. Consequently, I was frequently engaged in replacing worn out tracks, a task like some previously mentioned, and in spite of gender discrimination laws, definitely 'not for lassies'. Thus, even if I was not made rich, I was kept extremely fit.

The Tullochs themselves were pleasant people to work for. In time, I was appointed workshop foreman, but the grass, as always, is greener over the fence. I saw an ad for a plant inspector, applied, and got the job.

My main function was to see to the well-being of a fleet of

expensive excavators, large dump trucks and heavy bulldozers. No expense appeared to be spared on them, although otherwise, the tightest financial control was the order of the day. My company transport was an old-ish *Mini Traveller*, a distinctly vulnerable vehicle to travel in.

* * *

The company was also engaged in contract rock blasting in the oil-booming Shetland Isles. I had several trips there, travelling by air from Inverness, and then self-drive car. Shetland was fascinating and like a foreign land; it was at the height of its oil boom; accommodation and meals were excellent in the old style hotels. Its main snag was the seemingly constant rain, usually driving horizontally in the fierce winds.

A mile or two outside Lerwick, I was in a new workshop, overhauling a drill rig. At the end of the first day, the proprietor invited me to use his engineer's hand soap with the advice that since there was no water supply, I could break the ice on the pool outside the door and rinse my hands there – welcome nevertheless.

* * *

One of our young engineers was supervising and organising a big rock blast at a nearby quarry. He was physically a very big man and the following summer was trying to perfect the art of water skiing with no ski board, just on his bare feet. I didn't hear the outcome.

One day, he came to the workshop seeking my help on the quarry top. The driller had got one of his very expensive rock drills stuck down a deep hole on top of the quarry. As a drill progresses into rock, a series of extension steel tubes are screwed onto it to reach the required depth. When a drill is stuck, it is customary to 'blow' a couple of holes in the steel tube still protruding above the rock, then thread a length of steel rope through the holes. Often, following the blast, the drill can be retrieved undamaged. The 'blowing' incidentally is done using oxyacetylene flame-cutting equipment. This, the engineer wanted me to do there and then.

I have found that people accustomed to working with explosives appear to the uninitiated to be somewhat casual in the matter, although generally they know what is safe and what is not. I was not in that category; consequently I thought it prudent to have a 'look see' first.

At the scene, I could see extending in all directions from the steel tube, many tufts of polythene, etc., protruding from holes in the rock. Already knowing the answer, I turned to the engineer and asked, "Is this lot charged (with explosives)?"

Engineer: "Yes."

Me: "How much 'stuff' have you in it?"

Engineer: "About five tons."

Me: "Well, I think we'll unscrew the tube, take it to the workshop and do the job there.

He grinned and said, "OK."

My employment lasted about a year till I thought I had had enough. I was thankful to leave behind, what seemed to me, the oppressive rigidity of control. One of my last memories of it was the boss emitting a great sigh before uttering the most unexpected statement (from him), "I don't suppose that when it will come to the last ten gasps, it will matter how much money we made."

* * *

I was welcomed back to *Tulloch's*, but after some time, was again lured by substantially more money. My new job was connected with cabin cruisers. My very first task there was with a small team salvaging a sunken cruiser. My initial sight of it was about six inches of the prow above the surface – the vessel itself was in a nearly vertical attitude alongside an old pier at Foyers on Loch Ness side. A crane and a diver had been laid on and the vessel was slowly raised to the horizontal just clear of the surface, the water gradually pouring out from its hull through a large hole in the engine room area, originally caused by its having been allowed to drift onto rocks, unattended.

I was then required to strip out all the electrical components from its two engines for drying. Working fast, I had just about finished when there was a resounding 'bang', a lurch and water came pouring in through the hole in the hull.

The sudden reversal of affairs was caused by the overloaded crane sling snapping. I scrambled up through the hatch pretty quick, and made it onto the pier before my job disappeared back under water from whence it had come. Thankfully, in spite of all, the bottom line was success – the vessel was raised again, and with the hull temporarily patched, towed up the Loch by nightfall.

My new job certainly paid over the top, but there's a reason for everything and after two months, I was on the move again. If nothing else, over the years, my life has been full of changes. By the time I was sixty, I was employed by Wm. Tawse & Co., an Aberdeen firm, as buyer for plant and vehicle spares at their Inverness depot. Tawse paid minimum rates and once more it was a tight domestic budget.

My work desk was placed right against a window overlooking a large 'surfaced' area and adjacent to the workshop main door. On the whole, there was little excitement at Tawse, but one day I saw the entire workshop staff of eight or ten men evacuating the building at speed and gazing towards the big doors open-mouthed.

I went out to enquire what was happening to be told that an acetylene 'bottle' (cylinder) was on fire. I have never seen an exploding acetylene cylinder, but I believe it would be to say the least a sobering business. I had previously met a similar situation in Glasgow; then as now, those using the equipment seemed mesmerised, but also then as now, I hurried to it, quickly closed the gas valve and all was well.

* * *

I must be ever grateful to Rebecca over the period, insisting that our boys attend church every Sunday, and then to God the Creator of all things, that in their early teens, each of them was 'converted' – becoming firm believers in the Lord Jesus Christ as their

160

personal Saviour and Lord. A remarkable change came in the behaviour of the boys. Whereas before conversion they went to church unwillingly, afterwards they left our house eagerly, ahead of their parents.

Attending Dalneigh Church of Scotland with them, I grew rapidly in my Christian faith.

There are individuals I must mention in connection with our growth in the faith. Fergus Robertson the minister, Evan Cameron an elder – a most remarkable man who for 30 years that I know of, conducted his own prayer time at 7 PM every night at the church. I should think that in the thirty years, the number of nights he missed could be counted on one hand, and then he would have someone stand in for him.

My elder son Seoras was much encouraged in the faith by a young widowed schoolteacher, Jean Hogg, and when he was probably only about 14 years old, he started attending Evan's prayer times.

One day an old lady of the church Elsie Mackay waylaid me and told me, "He's all right now, Evan's praying for him," and as far as she was concerned that was his coming to faith, signed, sealed and delivered.

As it turned out, Elsie was right – Seoras married early, and before too long, he and his wife Elizabeth headed off for Bible school in Glasgow, stepping out in faith with no parental financial backing. They followed that with divinity courses at Aberdeen University, both taking degrees, and Seoras is currently a chaplain in the Army, all of which amazes me – for a less academic young man you couldn't imagine. I give thanks that, for what he may have lacked in academic fire, he more than made up for with a special gift of wisdom.

* * *

In the early 80s, the Inverness Evangelical churches organised an outreach campaign under the title 'Know Jesus, Know life', a clever pun I thought on the word know/no. There was a lot of preceding door-to-door work, an empty shop in the High St. open and manned all day for prayer, and several all night prayer sessions in Dalneigh church, resulting in probably the most wonderful time of spiritual blessing I have known. I am sure that during that period, many people became aware of their need to put their lives right with God in Jesus Christ and did so.

To my great joy, among them was my younger son Kenny, still only about 14-years-old. I was first made aware of it as I rolled slowly down Castle St. on my Honda motorcycle combination outfit. The Know Jesus committee had taken another empty shop as a coffee bar for 'outreach to teenagers'. Seoras was inside, saw me and dashed out to tell me, "Dad, Dad Kenny's become a Christian."

At some stage, Rebecca also had become a Christian. She told me that for some time she had been aware that Seoras and I had something which she didn't have, and one day, as she rode her bicycle down Fairfield Rd., a phrase of scripture suddenly flashed onto her mind and she knew that she must give her life to Christ.

* * *

As soon as our boys had reached an age when they no longer needed her constant attention, she had started work to help the meagre family coffers. She got herself a job as Deputy Matron at Inverness police station at Raigmore.

Matron duties consisted of feeding prisoners and cleaning the cell block. Thus she was on duty on alternate weekends, for relief at holidays, sickness and any other absences of the Matron.

When on duty, she had to be on the job at 7 a.m. We lived on the opposite side of town at Pict Avenue and three times daily, regardless of weather, she made the return journey by bicycle – a distance of 18 miles daily. Often, she carried hot food for her charges.

While she believed strongly in justice, she also had strong sympathy for many of those who had fallen foul of the law, and she was none to happy at the treatment unnecessarily meted out to them by some of the officers. At home, she prepared large pans of mince and mashed potatoes, which she carried to her 'unfortunates' in her cycle pannier bags. She was highly popular with the recipients.

On several occasions when on foot with her in town, we passed a little bunch of them and each time they hailed 'Mrs. Mac' warmly.

We did most of our about town travels by bicycle. Rebecca had a smart Dawes drop-handled bike, popularly referred to in our time as a 'racing bike'. It was not usual to see a woman of her years on such a machine; several times, as she passed groups of school children, there were excited cries of, "Look at the 'wifie' on the racing bike."

Rebecca on holiday at Stromness, Orkney Isles, 1979

Holiday campsite at Loch Dunvegan, Isle of Skye, 1981

Suzuki, successor to our Honda motorbike

I may have mentioned earlier, the practice in civil contracting of enhancing or achieving profitability through claims for extras after completion of the work. However just these might be, they were often strongly warded off by the client. Where I worked in Willia Tawse Ltd, claims were often pursued by a mature engineer, Ian Ross. Although we did not work together at all, during the 'Know Jesus' campaign, we got to know each other and that we were both Christians.

From time to time, Ian would come over to my office window and tell me he was on his way to a claims meeting somewhere, taking place at 3 p.m. and 'Would I please bear him up in prayer around that time'. On one important occasion his boss accompanied him and again the outcome was successful. Ian told me some time later that the boss said to him, "I don't know what your methods are, but you seem to get success where no-one else can." Psalm 25 in the Bible says: 'The secret of the Lord is with them that fear Him'.

There came a period of rapid changes in British industry, with frequent changes of ownership of viable companies. William Tawse like many others, changed hands with the usual accompanying redundancies. The engineer in charge of road surfacing, with whom I had no previous dealings, to my surprise came to me telling me that I was for the 'chop' – or I could accompany him to work in a cabin office based at Daviot, where a new owner *John Fyfe Ltd* of Aberdeen had asphalt and ready-mix concrete plants.

* * *

Life with my new boss Dennis was pleasant. The office staff was three persons – Dennis, his secretary and myself. I had managed to buy the most economical little vehicle I've ever had, a *Reliant Rialto* three-wheeled van, live rear axle and single-steering front wheel. This marvellous little vehicle was ideally suited for daily transport to Daviot. Because it was classed as a tricycle, I only paid 50% road tax – it was nippy and fuel frugal beyond belief.

Daviot is on high ground and, in winter, subject to significant snowfalls. John Fyfe's managers had smart Ford Sierra company transport. There had been a particularly heavy snowfall one day and it had been decided to quit work around 4 p.m. As I drove confidently away from our Portacabin, I passed a red-faced manager with several of his men feverishly trying to get his *Sierra* on the move. The *Rialto* was the 'bee's knees' for the snow.

Talk of snow reminds me of an occasion some years earlier, when the family had graduated to an old red *Mini* car, our first in Inverness. It was winter and we were visiting 'Granny' in Ullapool. Her son, Ian (Rebecca's brother), and his family were travelling by road from Rosehall area in Sutherland to visit at Ullapool.

It had been snowing and growing steadily heavier. Granny, a natural worrier, grew increasingly anxious, till finally I said I would head north to meet the travellers. The snow lay deep and as I progressed, I began to doubt the wisdom of my gesture. Passing Drumrunnie, the road ascended towards the snow-notorious Knockan Rock; the snow grew deeper and to my surprise, started to cascade up and over the *Mini's* tiny bonnet, as though being ploughed, but my hardy mount gave never a slip.

At Ledmore junction, I turned east, hoping to find my quarry at *Altnacealgach Hotel*. There, the hotelkeeper and his wife were shovelling snow from the entrance to their outbuildings. Somehow, the *Mini* turned and faced west, and I learned that the missing travellers had been there some time earlier, but had decided their best policy was to head back to whence they had come.

Still with the unusual sight of snow coming up and over the bonnet, I ploughed my way back to lower ground and eventually Ullapool.

Incidentally, translated from the Gaelic, the name *Altnacealgach* becomes 'The burn of deceit'. Tradition has it that in the far past, there was a land ownership dispute, one owner contending that the burn was the boundary of his territory. Eventually both parties agreed to abide by the verdict of a mutually acceptable referee. Unfortunately, the man who had been nobbled, lined his boots with soil from one side, walked well into the opposing terrain and swore the ground he was standing on belonged to the other side.

* * *

It was during my time at Daviot that I received a phone call from a former *Tawse* man who happened to work at premises next door to Rebecca's brother Willie's house.

The message was brief, "Come home immediately, your wife is very ill; you better hurry, it's pretty serious."

I was surprised to hear from the caller, because he was a man who previously, for reasons I've never fathomed, would not speak to me if he could avoid it.

Some days prior to this call, Rebecca had slipped on frozen snow, broken a bone in her leg and consequently was in plaster, considerably incapacitated, but otherwise in good health. As I drove home, I pondered what the situation could be, but was strangely at peace.

Entering the house I found Willie's wife, my sister-in-law, tidying in the kitchen. She looked at me and said simply, "She's gone. She's in the front room."

I went there and found my dear wife, sitting on a chair, apparently peacefully asleep.

There was a wonderful atmosphere of peace; we were both believers in the Lord Jesus Christ, and thus, to quote the Bible, 'We were not as those who have no hope'.

I kissed the cold brow, knelt on the floor beside her and gave thanks to God for her life. How long I remained there I cannot tell. Back in the kitchen, Jessie told me she had come in to visit and found Rebecca as she was. On later reflection, I realised that death had occurred prior to the phone call to Daviot.

That night I slept little. Sometime in the small hours, I was constrained to write down the following – which I later with difficulty read out at the start of the funeral service.

<u>3rd March 1989.</u>

Hello friends,

I wish on behalf of the family to sincerely thank you all for being with us at this time. On the morning following Rebecca's passing, I woke very early and I felt compelled to write what I could not entrust to my memory.

No doubt it is an unusual thing for someone in my position to be addressing you, but for many of you, it may be the only opportunity I will have.

Quite recently and without knowing how soon we were to be involved, Rebecca and I discussed the reasons for holding funeral services. Two reasons were immediately apparent – one to give thanks to God for a life we had known shared and loved. Secondly, hopefully to share with others, family, friends and acquaintances, something of the limitless riches we as individuals and as a family have enjoyed. Our wealth is not in pounds and pence, but in the sure and certain hope that God has graciously bestowed upon us – namely, the forgiveness of all our wrong thoughts, wrong words and wrong deeds – our sins, and the promise of eternal life in glory through our Saviour and Lord Jesus Christ. We do not boast, but in our sorrow we also rejoice.

We are grateful to have with us the Rev. John Ross and the Rev. Fergus Robertson, both better qualified than I to lead our thoughts, our prayers and our praise.

It is our great concern and it would have been Rebecca's, too, that we all listen very carefully to what God's men have to say.

For some, it will be joyful confirmation of what is already known to be true, but some of us will be clouded with sorrow, some, prisoners of unbelief, some with doubts, some even with objections, and some may never have allowed themselves to think of the issues before us, the issues of life and the issues of death. To all of you we say, put these things aside.

I quote to you some lines:

'Turn your eyes upon Jesus,

Look full in His wonderful face

And the things of earth grow strangely dim,

In the light of His glory and grace.

He is real.

He is alive.

He wants to give to each of us what He has already given
to me and to mine.

He is the way and the truth and the life.

It's not hard to learn about him.

It's all in His book.

Don't wait till sight and senses dim.

It's urgent.

Don't throw away your chance of the greatest free offer
ever made.

He says in His book 'Ask and you shall receive'.

That is a promise of God.

He does not break His word.

Memorial stone to Rebecca in Ullapool cemetery

People have asked if they could send flowers. We've had to say 'no'! They've asked whether there is some fund they might donate to, again we've had to say 'no'. What would have given Rebecca the greatest joy, would be the knowledge of lives given to following the same Master that she gave her life to. That way can produce a dimension of giving that pales flowers and money into insignificance, and the wonder of it is that the giver will receive far more than can ever be given.

Thank you all.

* * *

Because of the relatives, friends and acquaintances in both places, we were obliged to have services in Ullapool as well as Inverness. I still remember with gratitude the kindness of Mona Cormack, who had been a close friend of Rebecca's. She was adamant that on our return from Ullapool, the family must come to her for dinner. We enjoyed a delightful meal accompanied by quiet, sensible talk.

* * *

There followed a period of steady adjustment. In the space of just over a year, the household had altered from five persons to one. I received great kindness from a number of people. One family I must mention in particular, Sheena and Cathel Innes who repeatedly invited me to sumptuous Sunday dinners. Dennis, my boss at *Fyfe's*, was also extremely kind and accommodating.

Rebecca's mother, in advanced years, at Ullapool was totally broken and never really recovered. In old age, Rebecca had been her main stay. Gradually, I established a new but lonely pattern of life.

Time passed, there was a further *John Fyfe* take-over and Dennis *et al* were moved to new purpose-built offices at Beauly sandpit. I became a very busy man. In addition to my existing work, I now became the radio nerve centre for several road-surfacing squads who seemed to revel in crises situations, for many of which I had to find solutions.

Everything connected with asphalt road surfacing is very expensive and much more technical than might be suspected by those whose common view of the process is simply one more nuisance and smelly traffic hold-up. The material is under continuous temperature and content monitoring at both production and laying ends, entailing laboratory work and close attention from the client's inspector on site. Materials falling out of the tight parameters laid down were rejected and cost the contractor a 'mint'.

Reliability, or otherwise, of machinery could have drastic repercussions; most of my time tended to the 'otherwise'. Perhaps with good reason, I sometimes wondered how much of the trouble was contrived by those whose earnings would be increased by extending the working day with a breakdown.

* * *

I attained the 'magic' age of 65, when one becomes a 'senior citizen' and so eligible for state pension. Shortly before the day arrived, Dennis came to me asking if I could see my way to remain at work. Although I didn't reveal to him how much that would suit me, I agreed.

Now, for the first time in years, I had a worthwhile income – my earnings, plus a pension, and as a bonus, it's nice to feel wanted.

And then at church, I met Julia and somehow we 'clicked'. After a warm friendship, I popped the question and to my delight and some amazement, she was thoroughly in favour.

So began a new married life. Happily, my sons took readily to their stepmother. Now even as I write at the age of 78 years, the marriage has been running well for over twelve years.

* * *

Life ran pleasantly. From time to time there were cut backs at work; redundancies became commonplace. Some eighteen months went by and then Dennis came to me with solemn face.

"Hector, there are huge cut backs and you're on the list."

I said to him, "Well, that's OK, it's not a problem."

"Maybe not for you," he said, "but it is for me."

Again, it was nice to know that my efforts had not gone unnoticed. Dennis, I had to leave to what ever lay before him. For myself, I felt fit and I knew I still had useful work left in me. I had for some time been hearing quite a bit of the work of the *Blythswood* organisation. I phoned their office and was invited for interview.

With Julia – Wedding day
September 1989

Chapter 14

Blythswood

B *lythswood* is a Christian organisation, started many years earlier by the Rev Jackie Ross and others when they were divinity students in Glasgow. It was sparked off by the accusation that they expected people to come to their churches, but they never went to the people. Before long, the challenge accepted, they engaged themselves in visiting homes for down and outs in the city, bearing fish suppers and the Word of God.

Jackie's first appointment was to the little village of Loch Carron in Wester Ross and there he remained for the rest of his days. Sadly, after a long illness, he died of cancer at the age of 66.

I can only describe him as a dynamic Christian man who sometimes was guilty of sweeping practical problems away as if they didn't exist. He was the eternal optimist, but no doubt in true Biblical fashion, he laid the problems before God and left them there.

Towards the collapse of the Soviet Union, Jackie and other family members, hearing the reported persecution and privations of Christians behind the 'Iron Curtain', ventured into Eastern Europe, and I suppose what they saw was the catalyst for the scene into which I dropped.

* * *

Sometime in 1992, I met Jackie and his then lieutenant, a true Christian gentleman, Donald Macleod, at a café in Dingwall. There followed a barrage of questions, the final one being, "How much money would I want?"

On my reply that I had come as a volunteer, I was immediately appointed transport manager, responsible for I didn't really know what.

It was arranged I should meet Jackie next morning at the main depot at Alness. I arrived in good time to suss out what I had let myself in for.   There I found a large ex-RAF hanger, used for servicing flying boats in WW2.   Inside was stacked with mini-mountains of black plastic bags full of donated used clothing.   In pa clear space, a couple of women and one man, 'the manager', were sorting piles of old footwear into pairs.   I joined them to hear what the 'crack' was.   There was also a grotty old caravan, sectioned into a small office (mine to be) and a portion for a tea-room for the volunteers.

The ravages of fifty years had taken their toll on the hanger roof; when it rained, a good deal of it descended on the black bags inside – work spots had to be carefully selected.   In one corner lay a decrepit looking *Volvo* artic' truck, its trailer badly bent.   The hanger also had to serve as a repair and servicing depot for a fleet of six old *Volvo* artic' trucks, which, when money permitted, plied deep into Eastern Europe and Albania – all with volunteer drivers.

Hector with one of the fleet!

Someone once remarked to me that no-one in their right mind would go to the places your people go with these trucks.

Nevertheless, go they did and with amazingly little trouble. It says a lot for the quality of the *Volvo* trucks, not to mention that each departure was covered by Jackie's prayers with the drivers at departure and no doubt en route.

In addition, we had a motley assortment of lesser vehicles, mainly small vans. Our one struggling mechanic had a hard time, but we also had on tap a useful self-employed man who generally saved the day. I learned that some of the arctic' van trailers parked outside had been loaded with bags of clothing for some time, awaiting the day when money would arrive to send them on their way.

I often wondered what motivated drivers to undertake *Blythswood's* journeys for no visible reward, but Jackie was nothing if not persuasive and always brimming with confidence. From time to time, he took a trip himself, generally hastening back to fulfil his ecclesiastical duties.

One Saturday night, I had to open up the hanger for him arriving from far away – his eyes popping out of his head, having driven continuously for a number of hours, which it would be prudent for me not to record. He then had to drive close on sixty miles to Loch Carron and prepare for delivery of two sermons the following day.

Among our volunteers, we even had a retired General Surgeon who gave valiant service. Every time I think of his description of the day he qualified for a heavy goods driving licence, a smile comes to my mind. In his own words: "When I finished, the examiner said to me, "You've passed Mr. X, the important thing is for a driver to be safe, and you're safe."

(What the surgeon really quoted to me, the examiner, as saying, "You've passed, Mr X. But you're a terrible driver." Regrettably, he now strongly denies this.)

On a couple of occasions, the safe driver asked to borrow an outfit 'to practise reversing, because I'm not very good at it, Hector'.

* * *

175

Slowly, *Blythswood's* fortunes improved; the fleet of small vehicles grew steadily, each one little better than its predecessor; charity shops were established. A wonderful new asset was achieved. The RAF had left behind them an excellent transport building and somehow Jackie acquired its use. About the same time, our mechanic gave notice of his departure.

By advertising, we got hold of a replacement, the most competent I had ever encountered. A Clydesider, Davy Aird – in road transport, there was nothing that Davy could not fix – engines, electrics, bodywork, paintwork, the lot. It was not only fix, but also fix competently, so that you could rest assured only sound vehicles came from his hands, or from volunteers under his supervision. It was virtually unheard of that a 'Davy-prepared' vehicle would fail its MOT examination.

There was such an occasion when Davy had a complete old arctic' outfit in to the test station that was already scheduled for the Continent the next morning. It was failed for want of one official lead seal on the tachometer drive. The sealing could only be done at a government-approved garage, of which, at the time, Inverness had but one.

Davy hastened there, only to be told that the next available appointment was three days hence. As he made his way out through the garage, his sharp eye spotted a used seal lying on the floor. Since the seals are crimped on with special 'official' pliers that leave their imprint on the lead, seals can only be used once. Not so with Davy. In the passing, he scooped up the old seal, retired to a quiet spot, pried it open and crimped it in place using his own pliers. He returned to the test station and was promptly given his test certificate.

* * *

At the time of my arrival, the Bosnian war was in progress, so I was surprised to know that Bosnia was among our vehicle destinations. One driver on return told me of the trucks being rocked by close shell bursts, but no actual war damage was ever sustained.

Wherever there was need, Jackie sent the donations, which poured in from all over the country. His enthusiasm seemed to know no bounds.

One day I took a phone call from a gentleman in Glasgow seeking to borrow a Transit van to take medical supplies to St. Petersburg in Russia. I told him I would have to refer to Jackie and I would come back to him. I located Jackie at Loch Carron, filled in the scene for him and his immediate response was, "If we're going at all, we might as well send an artic', tell him we'll fill the rest of it."

Everything was to a very tight schedule; a volunteer driver, Bruce Georgeson, was delighted at the prospect. Quickly organised, he liaised with a vehicle from England bearing the medical goods, sped on to Harwich to catch a ferry sailing via the Kiel Canal to Gothenburg in Sweden, and motored across Sweden to Stockholm; from Stockholm another ferry across the Baltic to Turku in Finland; a further 300 miles across Finland, over the border into Russia and St Petersburg.

After leaving Alness, nothing further was heard from Bruce for about a fortnight. Then out of the blue came a Fax message confirming load delivery, and saying return might be delayed because 'Comrade Bruski of the Soviet division was house-moving a missionary couple from Finland to Harwich'. He returned without incident.

* * *

We need smiles in our life! Indeed, my wife Julia gives good advice on the subject: "When you see someone without one, give them one of yours."

At my *Blythswood* desk, I had some fairly difficult phone conversations. One pops into my mind. I was literally spelling out a lengthy double-barrelled foreign name to a young UK man.

All went well till we reached 'hyphen' – then came the struggling young voice, "How do you spell that?"

From time to time there were troubled phone calls from far away places, sometimes in the small hours.

* * *

I had reached the grand old age of seventy, but still reasonably fit. However, I started telling Jackie that it was time he had someone younger in the saddle. It took some time to convince him, but by the grace of God, a replacement was found in Finlay Mackenzie, and now the finances allowed the employment of a paid transport manager. Full marks to Finlay who gave up a 'secure' job to take over. He was familiar with what was needed, as he had already done a good number of *Blythswood* European trips himself. Probably about this time, another major and most welcome benefit took place in the appointment of George Dunn as full time financial controller.

* * *

Three years earlier, Julia and I had become involved with a young Ukrainian seaman, Oleg Serafimovich, who had been airlifted from a ship at Ullapool to our local Raigmore hospital for a leg amputation. Our initial contact was by a request that Julia would help him with the hospital menu, and 'could we find him a Russian language Bible?'

Since Julia had some knowledge of Russian, and *Blythswood* had Bibles, both needs were readily fulfilled. It was also provident that Trevor Foster, the hospital personnel manager, was fluent in Russian, not to mention a clutch of other languages.

We had sort of adopted Oleg and he soon left for his home port of Riga in Latvia and later, home. His meagre pay had stopped the day he left the ship, clad only in jeans and sweat shirt. He left Scotland with a new 'leg', a new wheel chair, money and well-kitted out from *Blythswood*. We received one or two short letters from him, and now one saying that things were not very rosy in

178

Kamienets-Podilsky, his home city in Ukraine; was there any possibility of humanitarian aid?

Oleg with Julia at Loch Ness

I was well into a hand-over period with Finlay, but I spoke to Jackie and he agreed with my proposal that I should take a trip to Kamienets-Podilsky. I did not hold a heavy goods licence, and so had to confine my transport to a 3½-ton *Mercedes* truck. Compared to the artic's, the *Merc* had seriously inadequate fuel capacity. The ever-resourceful Willie soon resolved the matter, spiriting up from the 'scrappies', two used twenty-gallon truck tanks complete with mounting brackets. He cut holes in the ends of the tanks, welded them together and mounted them on the *Merc*, making its range more than a match for the big boys.

Trevor's language skills had come from his twenty-odd years in the RAF and he was keen to accompany me. For a period in his service, he flew in the old Shackletons during 'The Cold War', monitoring the Russian radio transmissions and for some three years thereafter, served in the British Embassy in Moscow. It was arranged for Trevor to spend the night prior to departure with Julia and me. We were to rendezvous with another truck from Aberdeen at Ramsgate in Kent and catch the Sunday night ferry to Dunkirk, travelling together to Ukraine.

Leaving at five-thirty Saturday morning, we would have ample time for the ferry rendezvous. Heading for Perth, the first engine falters, and splutters came on the long climb out of Inverness. It cleared, we pressed on – 'we had only 4,500 miles to go'. The engine sickness came and went, making our progress rather slow. To turn back or not, that was the question. Leaving the Highlands and onto lower ground, the *Merc* seemed to have cleared its throat and sailing into Perth, our problem appeared solved. To make sure, I went to a commercial vehicle garage to check it. The verdict was, "Whatever it was, it's gone now, you're OK."

Three or four miles later, it returned with a vengeance, bringing us to a full stop. Our trouble was obviously fuel stoppage, although we were still carrying 35 gallons. I laboured in vain to resolve the problem; anxiety was starting to set in and I called base for help.

It takes time to effect a rescue from a hundred miles away – and on a Saturday afternoon. It was some three hours till the welcome appearance of Finlay and Davy.

Davy, familiar with the system he had rigged up, quickly bypassed it with nylon tubing into our tank and the Merc roared happily into life.

It was well after six p.m. when we set out again with some apprehension and some six hundred miles in front of us to Ramsgate. It was a rough ride, with driving wind and rain through northern England, till after a single stop for nature and nourishment, we fetched up near Newport Pagnell around 6 am, exhausted and with 180 miles to go.

A couple of hours sleep worked wonders; we pulled in at the next motorway services for the necessities of life. As we returned to the truck, enjoying the sunshine, we chatted with an old couple who were admiring the Bible verse on the side of the *Merc*: 'For

God so loved the world that He gave his only son that whosoever believes in Him should not perish but have everlasting life', (John 3:16). We motored on comfortably to Ramsgate, where later in the afternoon, we located the Aberdeen truck and its crew among the array of commercials waiting for the cheaper midnight ferry. We soon learned that our new travelling companions had done a number of aid trips with various organisations in the past.

Trevor and I were Christians, but they were self-confessed heathens, but it was OK they said: 'they had travelled with people like us before'. Ron, originally from Londonderry, was like myself, a former public works man, while John was a true Aberdonian ex-trawler engineer, bilingual – Doric and English. Between us we could muster English, Doric, Gaelic, Irish and Trevor's Russian, German, French, Norwegian and, I think, Swedish.

Our ferry passage had included a 'trucker-type' large free meal and we didn't intend to miss it. Thus with negligible sleep, half-past-one Monday morning found us in the mêlée of trucks in Dunkirk harbour area, and it was obvious that the sooner we were out of it the better.

One of the school subjects I had enjoyed was Geography. As we headed east, I was delighted to find that we would be coming to, if only bypassing, a string of cities memorable from school and wartime news bulletins – Ostende, Brussels, Liege, Aachen, Cologne, others less well known, then Dresden and, at last, Gorlitz at the Polish border.

We had lost Ron and John in Dunkirk and couldn't pick them up on our CB radio. The width of Europe from France to Ukraine lay before us either to find them or not, and I could foresee distinct difficulties if it was to be 'not'. We drove east praying, and some-where beyond Ostende around 4 a.m., we pulled in – shattered.

Reveille took place at 7.30; refreshed, we set off and by the grace of God, were soon in radio contact, quickly followed by visual contact.

Brugge, Gent, Brussels and Liege passed in their turn till just short of Aachen in Germany, we stopped in glorious sunshine for a substantial self-catered meal. Trevor and I did the honours from our copious supplies. Throughout the journey, our main course was always prepared in a single pan. This time, everything canned as usual, the menu was *Baxter's* Royal Game soup, chopped ham, potatoes and for good measure some *Heinz* beans, well heated and stirred together, followed by strawberries and coffee – very satisfying. As he lit up a cigarette, Ron asked whether a boy brought our morning paper as well!

Hector and Ron preparing lunch – Romania 1996

With typical practicality, the Germans had provided a pull-in with excellent concrete tables and benches for people like us. Even with driving on the 'wrong' side, the autobahns were a delight.

Ron and John, both employed by Aberdeen City Council, had persuaded the Council to hand over to them a redundant Ford arctic' unit which had lain rusting for years. Ron worked his magic on it and turned out an immaculate and resplendent machine. From somewhere, they dug up a suitable trailer. While it never gave a moment's trouble, its one bogey was its maximum cruising speed of 30 mph.

John, Ron & Trevor having navigation conference ~ 1996

Seven thirty p.m. and some forty miles east of Cologne, we came on excellent autobahn services and 'dropped anchor'. The sheer luxury of a shave, shower and the amenities of clean toilets were pure joy, followed by the sweet sleep of the exhausted. For most of the day both body and brain had been running mainly on autopilot.

* * *

At four thirty a.m., I wakened and sensed somebody outside. I switched on our sidelights and was amazed to see John standing in the open smoking a cigarette.

"What are you doing there, John?"

In best Aberdonian came the reply, "Ah michty (mighty), that man snores like a Rottweiler."

He was persuaded into our tilting passenger seat, wrapped in spare blankets and said all he needed was a bedtime story, which we delivered in the form of the Gospel; he had never heard it before.

* * *

On Wednesday, 325 miles took us to the Dresden area. The countryside was becoming distinctly Eastern Bloc, with new scenery and bumpy concrete roads.

A further early start 6 a.m. brought us to the German Polish border at Gorlitz at 11 a.m. – then, back six miles to the Customs post at Markers Dorf.

Trevor with his languages advanced to do his stuff – unfortunately, he didn't speak Polish. I accompanied him to the Customs office, a long room with seven or eight hatch windows, and several hundred drivers milling around in front of them, none looking too happy. Amongst them was a table with a ledger and two men seated at it. Ron and John, having no cab bunks, took advantage of the time by having a sleep in ours.

It was Trevor who sussed out that the ledger was the order of precedence for attention and it was carefully guarded by two waiting drivers. Having logged in at the register, he returned to the trucks with the news to 'come back at 10 p.m.' After another nourishing self-cater, at 10 p.m., he was advised to 'come back at 4 a.m.'

4 a.m. proved equally negative, but around seven, Trevor returned to the fray. At ten o'clock sharp, all the hatches banged down and mugs of coffee appeared, cigars lit up and the Customs men lay back, feet on desks. With patience strained, I wandered back to the truck park and, for something to do, counted some five hundred artic's, wagons and trailers waiting their turn.

Later, as I chatted with Ron and John, Trevor appeared with our sheaf of documents and looking distinctly downcast. Then came the reason, "It's no good," he said, "We can't go."

I asked him why?

He replied, "I don't know, I can't get any explanation from them."

Asking Ron John and Trevor in turn if they had any idea what we should do, I got three negatives.

"Right," I said, "We better speak to God about it."

Thus with bowed heads in the middle of the truck park, I put our case before the Lord. As soon as I finished, without another word Trevor took off towards the Customs office. Some time later, he returned, all smiles.

"That's it," he said, "As soon as I went in the office, a little Polish man came to me, speaking English. He said he had been listening earlier, and he explained what the problem was, all our documents had to be translated into Polish and he directed me to where I could have it done. We're clear to go."

Cost – a mere £37…to transit Poland, a further £55, plus road tax. Does God answer prayer? Yes, but in His time, not ours – and sometimes, His answer is 'no'.

The Polish roads started pretty bumpy, but then a sign indicating uneven surfaces for 25kms brought hope of better things ahead. The uneven surfaces turned out to be continuous potholes, reducing a seldom-achieved maximum speed to 20mph.

Our *Merc* was well sprung, but Ron and John's *Ford* was rock hard. Our hopes of relief after 25kms were soon dashed when the next sign indicated more of the same for 35kms. And so it continued right across Poland. In fairness, real asphalt surfacing was in progress on the other carriageway, but it was little help to us, and somewhere, we pulled up for another 'nosh' and rest.

As we progressed eastward along Route 4, the number of cities with unpronounceable names increased, accompanied by increasing air pollution from belching chimney stacks at Krakow. Tarnów, then Rzeszów (pronounce that one), the last town before the Ukrainian border, where we were met by armed soldiers and seemingly suspicion on every hand. It didn't help that the BSE crises was just petering out in the UK.

Were we carrying any meat? Of course we were, any amount of cans of various descriptions. Trevor brought his fluent Russian into play, but with little effect. Customs men and medical people tore open carton after carton, minutely examining the small print on the cans, till after long weary negotiations, we were allowed to advance within sight of the border barrier to have our papers dealt with.

The rest of us forced to be speechless, Trevor did all the donkeywork. From the other side of the barrier came a shout and there was Oleg, his wife, Angela, schoolboy son, Maxime, and two friends, Victor and Pavelle. I advanced to greet them, but was quickly driven off by a guard. After the application of many *shtamps* to the papers, we were eventually cleared through the barrier, to be greeted with bear hugs from Oleg. Having motored the ten-hour journey from Kamienets-Podilsky, they had been waiting 24 hours at the border.

It was now 6 p.m. and weary as we were, we went along with Oleg's requirement for an immediate departure. It soon became evident that the Polish potholes were as motorways compared with the Ukrainian 'roads'. We hadn't gone far till we came to a huge mound of gravel straddling the highway. On the level, it would have been impassable for trucks, but after some hasty talk between Trevor and our guides and since it was on a steep downhill, it was decided to have a go. Our guides' light car had no problem, next went Ron, his old *Ford* heaving like a ship in a rough sea, and so we motored into the long Ukrainian night.

Ron and John had by far the worst of the journey, being continually flung up off their seats, their heads often hitting the roof. We met the occasional ancient truck with the barest of lights and silencers long past any use, roaring mightily. Ahead, a single red light, which turned out to be the first of a number of level crossings with no barrier of any kind and negotiable only in first gear.

Weary beyond measure, around 4.30 a.m., we pulled up under trees in front of a very modern looking church building, journey completed. A waiting reception group opened up sheet steel gates of the churchyard and we drove inside. Fit young church men settled in to guard the vehicles for the remainder of the night and we were driven away to high rise flats where thankfully we fell into beds.

* * *

Nine o'clock-ish we were aroused for breakfast into a glorious 30 degree summer day. Eventually, unloading commenced under the watchful eye of the 'Tomashnovic' (Customs Officer). On completion, I was astonished to see the Customs Officer then 'seal' the large storeroom door in the church by simply driving nails at an angle through it into the doorposts.

I later learned that it was some two to three months afterwards before permission was obtained from Kiev HQ to unseal and distribute the goods.

By some means, we had been able to save from lockup and sealing, a specially designed Honda invalid tricycle for Oleg, other gifts for his household and also some cartons for the children's sanatorium.

At Oleg's bungalow, we were further greeted by his mother-in-law, Maria, and her sister Julia, two lovely old ladies, who anxiously saw to the washing of our hands; the otherwise tidy house had no running water. While Maria stood at the ready with soap and towel, Julia with a large pitcher rinsed us off into a chipped enamel basin on the floor. They were adamant we must have coffee with them, to our embarrassment accompanied by some of the biscuits we had brought for them. So moved was Julia that, biting her lip, she actually drew blood.

Our next call was at the sanatorium, a dismal building housing some twenty to thirty little children where it was obvious their mature nurse/attendants exercised love to them with the meagre resources and dated equipment they had. There we were introduced to sad little triplet girls, whom the nurses had dubbed Faith, Hope and Charity. Their picture was later well used by *Blythswood* in fund raising efforts.

Trevor introducing Oleg to his new transport

Triplets: Faith, Hope and Charity
At the sanatorium, Kamienets-Podilsky

On a later visit, I happened in when the little ones were having their afternoon snack. Solemn little faces, some daubed with *Gentian Violet* (memories of my own young days), they were sitting at scruffy little tables, having fruit juice out of old jam jars accompanied by small chunks of dry bread.

Teatime at the orphanage

A young legal interpreter Edward Domanski had been laid on for us. Through him we learned that Pastor Pilipuik was out of town, but was expected home at 6 p.m. and wished to speak with us.

By 6 p.m. my energy was distinctly flagging, but on arrival, the good Pastor engaged in continuous conversation with Trevor, while Edward kept me occupied with every conceivable question about 'The West'.

As midnight approached, I was again mainly on autopilot when Edward informed me that Pastor Pilipuik would like me to speak to the people at the service in the morning. "It will be in the cinema," he added.

"Why in the cinema?" I asked.

189

"Because it is the only place that can hold all the people."

"How many will there be?" I asked.

"Between five and six hundred, I expect," was the reply.

My mind went to church services at home in Inverness where fifty would be an excellent turnout.

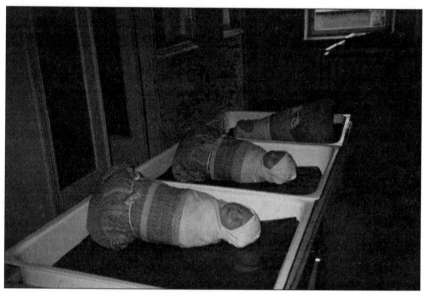

Production Line: Identity tags – old paste board and string

* * *

Sunday morning we were breakfasted (delicious smoked pork, coffee and big jug of apple juice), mustered and delivered to the cinema on time. By the grace of God, I managed to tell about Solomon, the Queen of Sheba, hard questions and with, hopefully, a parallel to the Lord Jesus Christ and the Way to the Kingdom of Heaven and its riches; three people 'repented'.

Among our 'aid' was a baby incubator, which led to our being introduced to Dr Natalia Chernish and given a tour of her large maternity wing of the General Hospital. There was a half built new wing with a rusty tower crane standing over it, abandoned some four years earlier. Inside, we were tickled at the high chef type hats worn by the male doctors. Our smiles quickly faded as we saw a rusty operating table, large areas of wall where the tiling had fallen off and a delivery room, primitive even to our unpractised eyes. The only likely-looking equipment was a pair of elaborate modern anaesthetic machines – that is, until they told us they were broken and unable to be fixed. Before we left, Dr Natalia was all but on her knees pleading that we should come back with supplies of nappies, syringes and needles.

There followed a superb meal in Pastor Pilipuik's house and then it was time for home. Between us we had delivered ten and a half tons of valuable aid.

* * *

Kamienets-Podilsky was much closer to the Romanian border than the Polish, and remembering the condition of the road from Poland, it was decided to try out the route home via Romania. Our little convoy was led by a guide car driven by Vovo from Pastor Pilipuik's 'Church of the Fifty' (Pentecost).

Crossing a lengthy bridge over the broad *River Dniester*, the sun was shining gloriously and suddenly disaster struck. Halfway across, Trevor and I at the tail end had lost sight of the others when a cloud of acrid smoke burst from our air vents and filled the cab. Both engine and vehicle had come to an immediate stop; as the smoke cleared, I managed to raise Ron on the CB and tell him our situation. There followed an urgent prayer to God for help.

I had managed to undo the dashboard and lay bare what was behind it. I was somewhat shocked to find a wiring loom of many wires frazzled in total melt down, an electric relay burned out, and for good measure, a vital nylon air pipe had melted through.

Vovo, realising there was no one following him, had about turned to see what was happening. He arrived and Trevor explained at length to him our situation. His response was a hand raised on high and the words, "OK OK, niet probliem, Slava Bogoo," words which we heard many times in Ukraine.

191

Translated, they mean: 'No problem, praise God'. To Trevor and me, there was a very distinct problem, as we watched Vovo and his car disappear into the distance.

* * *

Apart from our 'probliem', the scene was idyllic – lovely green countryside, the river placid well below us, and swimmers making full use of it, or sunning on its banks. Something made me move our three cameras and stuff them under a sleeping bag on one of the bunks. Trevor out in the open had started catching up on his neglected diary when I noticed two pistol-packing policemen heading our way.

As they arrived, the elder of the two immediately put his English into practice.

"Vat iss this you write. You are spies, ve vatch you, you are diplomat spies. Where the cameras, binocular, ve see you?"

Before anyone could reply, he lunged into the cab to search, while his companion smiled sweetly – and I prayed earnestly in the name of Jesus.

He searched the cab high and low, everywhere, except under the vital sleeping bag, not a camera or binocular to be found.

Meanwhile, Trevor searched feverishly through our file of many documents till at last he managed to locate the one from the Ukrainian Embassy in London which advised that we had come with humanitarian aid and were to be given every assistance. Our man read through it at length, grunted, thrust it back to Trevor and he and his companion stalked off back to their post at the far end of the bridge – sighs of relief and so much for the assistance.

But assistance came all right. We were heartened to see the car that had met us at the border arrive, driven by Pavelle, Pastor Pilipuik's son, and with him, another young man of short stature. Trevor explained to him what had happened, he had a squint in the cab and announced, "Niet probliem."

He went to the boot of his car and withdrew a bag of tools followed by a large sheaf of tangled up second hand cable. I was far from sharing his confidence with the 'niet probliem', but it turned out to be fully justified. We stood back, as he installed himself in the cab and went to work.

Our *Merc* wiring had the common *Lucar* terminals, which are of the 'use once' variety'. They cannot be used a second time. One by one, our expert, for such he was, separated each wire in turn, patiently pried open its *Lucar* terminals and reused them on cable lengths from his bundle.

He was doing so well that, eventually, Trevor asked him, "What about the burned relay and the nylon tube?"

Another 'niet probliem' – a specialist would come.

True to his word, Vovo returned bringing with him another man with a neat attaché case – the specialist. We now had an expert and a specialist at work.

The electric work completed, the specialist set about the nylon air tube. It was melted through about two inches from its connection to the air pressure gauge. He undid the connection and from somewhere down in the chassis, he dug up spare slack allowing him to cut off the damaged part. Nylon tube connections are made using brass ferrules, which are crimped (squashed) onto the tube and 'definitely' cannot be reused.

But our specialist did. He then summoned me over and showed me a tail of wire dangling from the dash end and a loop of wire passing below the steering column, a small part in the middle bared of insulation. He touched the loose end to this part; the starter immediately engaged, the engine fired up and the air pressure started to rise. Hallelujah, we were mobile again.

As our rescuers tidied up, I asked Trevor to tell them that we wanted to pay now. The reply was, "Christian brothers do not pay."

The only reward we could offer was a tin of excellent mechanic's soap, with which they were delighted as they washed their hands in the river below. On a later visit, I brought them each a nice big kit of autospark's, terminals, etc.

With profuse thanks and goodbyes we lined up behind Vovo and headed for the Romanian border. The whole exercise had taken about four and a half hours. At home at the appropriate garage, it may have taken nearer four days and probably four hundred pounds.

* * *

We cleared the Romanian border control at Siret in the small hours with little trouble, motored a bit and parked outside an all-night café with wild disco music, and not even that deterred us from sleep. Our mission was accomplished and we were on the home run.

Monday, much more relaxed we headed west. Romanian roads didn't have much to recommend them; at a couple of industrial parts, the air pollution was chronic. Traffic was light, a scattering of cars, horse and ox-drawn wagons, intermixed with the odd heavy transport.

Our route took us through the beautiful terrain of Transylvania and high in the Carpathian Mountains, we came upon a lone old man, virtually in rags. As we came face to face, he greeted us with handshakes, hugs and warm eastern European smackers.

We fixed him up with what we could spare from our own clothes, food and twenty cigarettes from Ron or John. He must have thought it was the day God opened a door in heaven for him.

Lovely green valleys followed, where docile black and white cows wearing large wooden 'bells' grazed contentedly, and after another self-cater of delicious home-cured pork from Ukraine, in the evening we fetched up in Cluj Napoca.

It was in Cluj that *Blythswood* had centred its Romanian activities, run by Rona Mackenzie from Loch Carron. Already armed with Rona's flat address, we hired a taxi to guide us there.

Dana, whose flat it really was, insisted we stay the night, in spite of already having two guests, Jackie Ross and Jamie, cameraman from Tern Television. Somehow, we all found shakedowns, even if Jamie slept outside on the balcony. I was told later that Jamie was so impressed with what he saw of Christianity in Romania, that, when he got home, he bought and read a Bible, joined a church and became a Christian.

In the morning, we had a quick visit to Jackie's new project, the Daniel Centre, still building and to be a home and skills teaching place for Romanian lads who had outgrown their orphanages and simply been turned out to fend for themselves.

* * *

A seventy-mile-run took us through the city of Oradea and to the Hungarian border, then Budapest and onto the superb toll M1 motorway that traverses westward from Budapest.

Suddenly there was a 'mighty rushing wind', a violent storm with torrential rain. As it eased, off I was aware of a *Blythswood* arctic' hammering eastwards. I had just a fleeting glance of the driver, Jimmy Stewart, the placid Irishman whose more usual occupation was collecting loads of donations around Scotland.

Bypassing other intriguing names, Tatabánya and Győr, our night stop was at the Austrian border.

The Austrians have a thing about fuel tax; every commercial vehicle entering has its tank contents checked and for everything over 200 litres, tax has to be paid.

Almost into Western Europe with still a little money in our kitties, we were feeling more upbeat and indulged ourselves with an autobahn services meal.

At some point en route, there was a bit of a CB debate taking place about our navigation when I was surprised to hear an English trucker voice cutting in saying, "Linz is to the left…where is it you want to go to?"

We were now making cracking good time; we were knocking off over 600 miles a day.

* * *

Nine p.m. on Thursday 30th May saw us back in Dunkirk. We sailed on the 11.30 p.m. ferry and tucked in to the standard truckers' free meal.

Rolling again in the small hours on Friday, sleep, or rather the want of it, forced us to a halt near Canterbury at 3 a.m. Noise from the morning traffic brought us to life again and underway at 6.30.

Ron and John were anxious to be back in Aberdeen early and had gone their own way. We contacted base and were instructed to make two donation collections. The first was at Knutsford Services on the M6. There, Brenda Forshaw, a stalwart *Blythswood* volunteer met us with the material, delicious coffee and sandwiches.

Next stop was at the home of Arthur and Moira Ness, a lovely Christian couple in the Lake District. Their giving included an excellent hospital operating table and the welcome pleasure of a real bed for the night.

A further long day's motoring and the truck was back in base at 5 p.m. on Saturday. In our 15-day journey, we had covered 4,463 miles, been in 10 countries and come home with £12.60 change from our expenses.

Looking back at my notes of the trip, I read that it was exhausting, enlightening, stressful, humbling and spiritually profitable.

* * *

Of Kamienets-Podilsky, I've written: Beautiful city, churches, fortress, Mafia, pig, cherries, grapes and strawberries. The huge pig, destined eventually for Pastor Pilipuik's table, lived in an immaculate mosaic-tiled sty at the back of his bungalow, where we also enjoyed the succulent cherries, grapes and strawberries.

The fortress was ancient and fascinating; it had rusted cannon balls projecting from its wall from a siege in the far past. Inside, was a touching war memorial and an enormous treadmill (for men) that was used to raise water through a shaft in the rock from the *River Smotrych* far below.

War Memorial in the old fortress

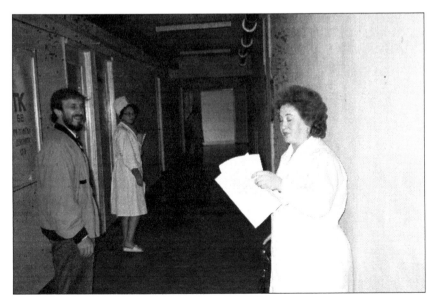

Pastor Koval and Dr Natalia Chernish in the hospital

My notes are headed with a Bible quotation from *James 2:15-16*. "Suppose a brother or sister is without clothes and daily food. If one of you says to him, 'Go, I wish you well; keep warm and well fed', but does nothing about his physical needs, what good is it?"

* * *

Now with diminishing hours, I continued daily at *Blythswood* till 19th September 1997, when I again set of for Kamienets-Podilsky – this time, with nappies, syringes and needles – thousands of them for Natalia Chernish's maternity unit. As she stood watching them being unloaded, she was biting her lip so hard, I feared she would draw blood, as I recall Oleg's Aunt Julia actually did when we took gifts into her house.

I was alone in my vehicle, but accompanied by a *Blythswood* truck headed for Odessa, driven by James Cannon. This time, we routed through Hungary via Budapest and more fascinating names, Szolnok, Debrecen, Nyíregyhása, to the border at Záhony and on the Ukrainian side, Cop. No vehicle park this time; it was mid-afternoon on the 25th when we joined a long vehicle queue on the two lane main road; we couldn't even see the border controls.

I was struggling to stay awake, but from time to time, the queue moved forward a vehicle length, sometimes two or three. If one didn't follow closely, the vehicle behind would overtake and fill the gap. The hours trickled by till day became night and very dark.

A knock at my driver's door – a young lady of the night plying her 'wares' escorted by a formidable looking matron. In Hungary, they were on open offer along the main roads by the gypsy camps.

Throughout the night there had been no possibility to sleep. At the border, vehicles were directed by ominous looking characters wearing black tracksuits and wielding long batons.

The proceedings were protracted beyond reason. Another day, and it was dark again when we cleared the Hungarian system. At some point I had written in my diary: 'Dying of fatigue and hunger'. Exceedingly weary, we had to wait while a sizeable convoy assembled, then led by a Ukrainian army truck, we got under way, and headed for the Ukrainian border control.

We hadn't gone far when out of the darkness I was amazed to hear loud calls of 'Meester Hector, Meester Hector' and there was Oleg, waiting who knows how long. He was a welcome passenger and his presence and language capability helped us through the Ukrainian system. Altogether, it had taken 34 hours to clear from one country into the other.

* * *

It was 1 a.m. when we cleared the border, and at the first fuel facility, we stopped for fuel and a brew of coffee. I have used the word 'facility' because that's all that it was. The norm in Ukraine at that time was a big square tank up on blocks, having a flow meter and gravity feed.

We demanded of Oleg that we must sleep It was 1.45 a.m. when he reluctantly agreed, with the words, "OK, we leave at four."

And so it was, setting off again on the 250 miles to Kamienets-Podilsky. The obvious route was due east, but whether because of road conditions, the mountains or bandits I know not, instead we took the five-hour route north-east to the city of Ternopil, followed by a further five hours south-east to Kamienets-Podilsky.

This time I was greeted by new acquaintances, Pastor Vladimir Koval and an interpreter, Vasyl Vasylovich Troian (Basil son of Basil) Troian. Vasyl and I later became close friends. He worked as a teacher of English and German in one of the city's six high schools. For his labours, he received the equivalent of $25 per month. On this, he struggled to raise his two children, his wife having died of cancer some years previously. Vasyl had been an officer in the Soviet army and had twice turned down invitations to join the KGB.

Soon, I was fixed up with a single-bedroom flat to myself; it was 11 p.m. when that truth dawned as I was handed the key by its normal occupants, Victor and Svetlana. At eight next morning, they returned from in-laws to prepare breakfast for me.

On my earlier visit, Pastor Koval had come to me after the service in the cinema. He had handed me a letter in Russian requesting general help and help to build an Evangelical church. By virtue of generous help from *Blythswood,* he has now done this.

Pastor Koval – foundation of new Prayer House ~ 2000

It was on this trip that, on Sunday morning, I attended the double wedding of two of Pastor Pilipuik's daughters. Vasyl sitting next to me in a pew instructed me on Ukrainian etiquette. "When congratulating the couples, remember you will kiss the men and shake hands only with the ladies."

A touching moment in the service was when each spouse in turn was handed a PA microphone, knelt down and prayed aloud for God to bless their union.

On Sunday evening, I attended Pastor Koval's service, held in the former communist 'reading room' – the ground floor of a high-rise block. Its drab grey interior softened somewhat when, at the end of the service, the Pastor read the closing verses of the book of *Acts, Chapter 20,* which refers to the Apostle Paul's departure from the city of Ephesus. Verse 37 reads: 'They all wept as they embraced him and kissed him'. A schoolgirl thrust a great bouquet of flowers into my hands and there were few dry eyes (including mine), as even rough bearded men gave me similar treatment.

At the hospital, Dr Natalia Chernish laid on a special afternoon tea to which the 'Tomashnavic' was also invited. He had, of course, been in close attendance throughout the unloading. Dr. Natalia said it was the first aid she had ever had; the hospital had nothing new for 15 years. Those who complain about our NHS hospital food might reflect that in 'KP', patients' food has to be brought in by their families. I waited impatiently for James' return from Odessa, but by Thursday, I knew I must leave on Friday morning without him.

My urgency was because it had been arranged that on Saturday I should meet an American missionary, Jim Johnson, in Prague and house-move for him back to Blantyre in Scotland.

On the Thursday evening, Vasyl said to me, "Tomorrow, Pasha will take you to the border. He was a criminal, highway robber, but he has repented."

On Friday morning, having said my goodbyes, I was introduced to Pasha – tall, lean and with a fair bit of English.

Ten or a dozen miles out of town, I was signalled to stop by a man in soldier's kit and using a police black and white striped baton.

"Stop, Pasha?" I asked.

"Niet, niet" came the answer, "Evil man, take money…go, go."

A lot can be said in ten hours; gradually Pasha's story came out. Briefly, having asked Pastor Pilipuik to marry him to a Christian girl, Oksana, because he was not a Christian, Pastor Pilipuik refused. In Pasha's words, "I was very angry, I went home, I got a Bible and read it, and I repented and believed. After we married, Oksana was expecting a child. At six months, she had severe pain in her back. At the hospital, it was diagnosed as tuberculosis of the spine and she must not have the child. We were very sad, we told it in the church and the people prayed over her. When she went back to the hospital, the doctors could not find anything wrong and they could not understand it."

Oksana produced a healthy boy and since then has had three more."

Pasha followed up his conversion with three years in Bible College. I have heard him preaching and although I couldn't understand a word, I must say, it was obvious he spoke with fire. He earns a living building stone fireplaces.

Oksana & Pasha

At the border, I tried to give him some Ukrainian money I had left over, but he refused my every effort. Then suddenly, he asked me for it, disappeared for a bit, returned and thrust American dollars into my pocket, which he had exchanged it for. He still had to make his way 300 miles home.

It was a particularly dark night with minimal illumination from the eastern yard lighting. When we had been struggling with the Customs, an old customs man had come to our rescue and rattled us through the system. We had just got into our van when Pasha announced, "Moment, moment," dived into his grip bag and fished out a New Testament. "Gospel, customs man," he announced and disappeared into the night.

It was the last thing I needed, as we were again in an escorted convoy. At the last moment, Pasha returned breathless.

"Did he take it?" I asked.

"Da, da (yes)," he replied.

"What did he say?"

He said, "I do not believe," and I said to him, "**Why you do not believe?**"

Thus, we parted company and by 00.30 a.m., I was on my way to Budapest.

* * *

By the grace of God, my eyes stayed open and my brain awake, but only just. At 5.00 a.m., I pulled into a services parking area near Budapest and collapsed into deep sleep in my driving seat; there were no bunks.

At 8.30, I wakened, had a quick wash, etc., a breakfast of corn flakes, muesli, raisins and UHT milk and headed, as I thought, for Prague.

Two hours later, I noticed the road signs saying 'Belgrade'. I figured I had the right road number but the wrong direction.

A bit deflated, I turned about and headed north and west. Hours later, just short of the Austrian border, I turned off for Bratislava in Slovakia.

Bratislava is a name that had long fascinated me; unfortunately before reaching it, I had to turn off again for Czech Republic and Prague. While the Slovak border people were no bother, not so with the Czechs, but after some indecision, I was on the long and excellent road to Prague.

As arranged, I rang Jim Johnson from the first *Macdonald's* in Prague (there are four of them) and soon we were enjoying a hearty *Macdonald's* platter together. There followed a most welcome bath and plenty sleep at his flat. Jim's wife and children were already in Blantyre; his lease had ended, so a quick load up on Sunday morning and we were off.

* * *

We stopped for fuel and a meal near the German border, everything half the price – it would be in Germany. Our stew was tasty, but the nearest thing I've experienced to stewed rope.

Out at the van again there was a sheet of paper stuck under the wiper blade. I am not keen on that kind of thing because often it is not good news. This time it simply said, 'Greetings, all the way from Dornoch', which is a small town in the north of Scotland. I have never traced the writer.

For some reason, Jim was anxious to reach his destination as quickly as possible; he volunteered to share the driving and to my relief, he turned out to be competent. Our only stops thereafter were for meals, nature and a short delay waiting for the ferry at Ostend, which by God's grace turned out to be a fast catamaran, cutting the crossing time in half.

We had motored with minimal pause all day Sunday, Sunday night, Monday, till around 11.30 p.m. we were in the Blantyre area.

Unfortunately, Jim didn't know how to find the peculiarly named Crossbasket Castle, the UK headquarters of his 'Latter Rain Ministries'. After two enquiries and 'Never heard of it, Jocks', I was getting in the van when in his thick American accent, he said, "We'll be there in five minutes."

A little 'fragile' with weariness, I responded, "God willing, Jim, we'll be there in five minutes."

With what sounded like rebuke and a touch of indignation came, "I've just asked in the name of Jesus" – and who could argue with that?

I had driven about three minutes when I came to a fork in the road. I stopped and said, "Right or left, Jim?"

Before he could answer, I was aware of a car stopping beside me; the driver came over and in a broad Lewis accent, "You look very lost, what are you looking for?"

Myself: "Crossbasket Castle."

"Ah well, you're two minutes from it, just follow me."

So it was, five minutes indeed, followed by a warm welcome and an even more welcome comfortable bed for the night.

In the morning, some breakfast, unload, a collection to be made from *Blythswood's* Glasgow depot and an easy drive home. Halfway to the Glasgow depot, I was stopped in a police check.
Policeman: "Where have you come from?"

Myself: "Prague."

Policeman: "All right, carry on."

I shouldn't think he had many from Prague that morning.

* * *

After that, life went on fairly quietly, well nourished with Julia's high-grade cuisine and a daily little input to *Blythswood*, till I was offered another trip to Ukraine. This time I was to have Billy McQuillan for a mate in the old *Merc* truck and accompanied by my old buddies Ron and John in a *Blythswood Volvo* arctic', both trucks with the luxury of bunk sleeping accommodation.

I am not a diary man, but for these journeys I kept a diary of sorts, and my mind boggles as I review our first three days schedule, based of course on gaining the benefit of cheap late night sailing. The notes run:-
Depart Deephaven depot (Evanton)   05.15 hrs   02.05.98

Arrive Bothwell Services   (statutory rest break) 19.00 hrs
02.05.98. 187 miles
Depart Bothwell   20.05 hrs   02.05.98
Arrive Welcome Break Services, (rest break) 23.40 hrs 02.05.98.
Depart   00.45 hrs   03.05.98
Arrive Chorley Services   02.47 hrs   03.05.98
Depart   10.00 hrs   03.05.98

                         Etc.

Arrive Ramsgate Ferry Terminal   16.00 hrs   03.05.98

At Ramsgate we met up with Ron and John and shortly afterwards, we were joined by Bob Taylor, his son Raymond and a
friend just out for the run. Bob had resurrected a mighty and
ancient tractor unit and trailer, which had been lying in a field.
His outfit was plated for 70 tons Gross weight, although on this
trip, it was possibly half of that. He was headed for Donetsk in
Ukraine with aid for an organisation called *Eurovision*. He had
never been on the continent before and was keen to be in convoy
with us.

John, Ron & Trevor at Ramsgate Ferry Terminal

It was the usual Sunday midnight sailing that actually departed at one o'clock Monday morning, the big truckers' tuck in and Ostende at 5.30 a.m., 6.30 Continental Time.

Then, it was the big rush to clear the horrors of the Brussels ring road before the morning peak traffic.

More long drives, good roadside noshes, a couple of minor navigational errors, somewhere loosing Ron and John on the way, and we made Görlitz customs by 13.30 p.m. on Tuesday. By the grace of God, the lost ones rolled in ten minutes after us.

It seems remarkable to me that heavy trucks can roll across Europe so close to each other for the best part of 24 hrs, including an overnight stop, and yet not see each other. On comparing notes, we found that we had shared the same truck stop park overnight.

This time, Görlitz went smoothly and in six hours, we were through, the delay simply being due to the volume of traffic and consequent queue. Things had improved a lot in Poland from my visit of two years before.

That evening we reached a good truck stop with excellent toilet facilities. To save our foreign currency we had our usual self-cater, followed by showers, etc.; for 5 Zlotys apiece, the whole team was thoroughly 'hygiened'.

Next morning, reveille was at 5.50, wash, kettles boiled and by ten to seven we were rolling. There was good progress to the outskirts of Kraków, then there was some bother in the form of a damaged bridge with a 7½-tonne load limit and a diversion. Both routes were sign posted Przemyśl, the last Polish town on our route. Two of us took the diversion while Bob Taylor with his 30 (plus) tonnes, successfully crossed the 7½-tonne bridge and was temporarily lost.

Recalled by CB radio, Bob again crossed the taboo bridge and rejoined us on a Kraków road, but alas, our sense of direction had gone. Once more, we had recourse to prayer and in minutes a Polish man with a scant smattering of English came to us. After complex and unsuccessful verbal directions, he said if we wished, he would bring his taxi and guide us onto the main road east again, but we must pay by his meter.

Taking us by an 'impossible' route, he stopped and pointed east. I sat in his taxi and paid his bill of $30, which was value for money split in three. As I heard his engine start – to leave – with sudden shock, I realised I had left my precious wallet in his taxi. Virtually without pause, the engine stopped and he popped out holding aloft my wallet. I can only say thank God for an honest man and a God who looks after me.

Clear of Kraków, we found a good lay-by in which to eat. With Billy McQuillan as chef, full justice was done to a starter of canned fruit followed by corned beef, potatoes and sweet corn – pronounced excellent by all. There was still about 230 kms to the Ukrainian border, and at 6.40 p.m. it was decided to 'go for it' that night.

Bob Taylor had an arrangement to rendezvous at the last filling station in Poland, with a *Eurovision* guide from Donetsk. Which was the last filling station? They were few and far between. At around ten o'clock, we came on one and weariness told us that would have to be it, right or wrong. For some reason, Bob took a turn of considerable anxiety about his rendezvous. Before turning in, I tried to reassure him, telling him that we were tired, it would be all right in the morning and that Billy and I would pray about it. I think unconvinced, he left me.

At eight o'clock next morning, there was a knock on his cab door and there stood a smiling Alexy and his pal Sergy from Donetsk. Billy and I had a book of *Spurgeon* daily readings with us. Each one had a short profound heading phrase. The night before, it said: *Never seemeth serenity so pleasant as following alarms.* It was based on the book of *Job.*

We felt it so apt for us that I called Ron on the CB and read it out to him. He was so intrigued, that although a self-confessed heathen, he wanted to know more and I had to give him some inklings of the story of *Job,* mentioning of course, Satan's meeting with God. I wasn't aware that John was not in the cab with him at the time.

I was wakened in the morning by a call on the CB. It was Ron wanting me to tell the story again for the benefit of John. Not yet fully awake, I was having difficulty understanding what he was on about, but he got the message through with the following – 'You remember that time when Satan was *newsing* with God' (sic).

Alexy had for transport, a very passable minibus, I suspect financed from America. He took us through the border system in a mere three hours. Later I learned that he had paid $25 to do so – *Blythswood* has a strict 'no bribes' rule.

Billy had managed to arrange 50 Gideon Russian language New Testaments for us to take. At the border, they went like snow off a dyke. In no time, they were eagerly accepted by all types, including the Customs men. People were reaching out of their cars for one.

Alexy had arranged a meal for us at the flat of a Christian lady in the city of L'vov. She wasn't able to be present, but had left all the necessities.

Two hundred kilometres later at 10.30 pm, we stopped for the night just outside the city of Ternopil, where Bob Taylor would part with us for Donetsk. Before bedding down, it was noticed that his giant truck had developed a radiator leak. The problem was quickly resolved by the addition of half a dozen egg whites to the cooling system.

Sound asleep at midnight, there came a knock on our cab door and there was Oleg, Angela and Maxime, his wife and son. He should have met us at the border, but apparently had big problems with water in the petrol of his little car – a not uncommon thing in Ukraine. I recall also one time getting a tank full of diesel fuel with a hefty peat content, which also created problems.

* * *

A long haul south with Oleg guiding and we received a warm welcome in Kamienets– Podilsky. Ron and John headed back for home ASAP. On the Sunday, Billy and I were guests of honour at Pastor Pilipuik's morning service, which was crowded right out the doors. I brought some amusement to the congregation when handing over various monetary gifts. As usual, Julia had primed me with one or two useful Russian words and phrases. She had also given a small gift to give to the Pastor's wife.

Endeavouring to show even a slight knowledge of their language, I handed it over, announcing it was from my 'sheena' (wife) for his 'sheena'. I noticed an immediate change in facial expressions, accompanied by smiles and chuckles in the congregation. I later learned the correct word for wife is 'sheenagh', while a 'sheena' is a motorcar tyre.

The road travel distance from Kamienets-Podilsky to UK is not greatly different, whether travelling via Poland or via Romania. I had learned that a new church was imminently opening in north-western Romania, and Billy and I had decided we would try to attend at the event. The location was at a village – Popeşte, near the town of Marghita.

It would be the first-ever Evangelical church in Popeşte and the village had one only Christian man in the last 40 years. Finlay Mackenzie of *Blythswood* was familiar with the area and with Baptist Pastor Dan Micula of Marghita whom God had used for the project. Dan had the vision, a lady from the Dingwall area had provided money to buy ground, American Southern Baptists had provided an excellent prefabricated church building and Swedish Christians had provided the furnishings.

We arrived in Marghita Town Square on a sunny Thursday after-noon. Unable to find Pastor Dan's house, we prayed for help. Every bench in the square had occupants relaxing in the warm sunshine, but none spoke English. Finally, a prayer of desperation and I felt a hand gripping my arm. There was no attempt at conversation, only the hand's owner leading me away across the square, while the vodka fumes from him might have caused an explosion.

We turned out of the square into a broad gravel road and I started to doubt my wisdom in going further with my guide when we stopped before a large house with a high steel security fence. Prolonged pushing of an electric bell button eventually resulted in the arrival from the back of the house, of a tall, well-built, serious-faced man with iron-grey hair, black clerical clothes and dog collar. His appearance reminded me strongly of the Highland Presbyterian ministers of my childhood.

He introduced himself in perfect English, "I am Laslau Fasakas – in your language, Leslie Potter, Presbyterian Pastor of this town, can I help you?"

Help us he did, sorting our problem quickly. He was Hungarian and had studied theology in St. Andrews University. As we parted, he handed me a small card with a name and a Scottish telephone number.

"When you get back to Scotland," he said, "Will you please phone this number and rebuke my friend, Rev.----, for not writing to me."

I carried out his request as gently as possible, his friend protesting how busy he was.

* * *

Dan Micula and his wife Lidia welcomed us warmly, their house was full up, but we could park and cab-sleep in their back yard. Sometimes, I think we don't really appreciate how well off we are in this country. Every house was surrounded with a high steel security fence, and we were invited back for a wash when the town water supply would be turned on at 9 p.m.

The building of Popeşte's 300-seat church was itself something of a miracle. Despite a hiccup in the foundation plans, as all arrangements had been made for the opening, the erection of the building, attractive white fence and laying out of the tidy front area was completed in eight days, start to finish. On Friday and Saturday, Billy and I gave what help we could.

211

At 5 a.m. on the morning of the Sunday Opening Service, Pastor Dan had to awaken the exhausted workmen sleeping in the church.

As seems usual in Eastern Europe, the service was at 9 a.m. To assist with the Praise, there was a detachment of 40 male choir singers from the choir of 230 at a large Baptist Church in the city of Oradea. The service lasted four hours, with three sermons, and although I did not understand a word, it seemed more like an hour.

* * *

The Swedish Christians had acquired the former Communist officials' holiday camp in the nearby 'Black Forest' where they had set up a trades' training camp for youngsters grown out of their orphanages. There we had a celebratory meal. The one Popeşte Christian produced a piano accordion, sat down with the choir members and to my amazement, struck up in Romanian, the well known hymn Amazing Grace.

At the evening service there was an invitation for someone from Blythswood to speak. Since there appeared to be no takers, I felt obliged to show willing. I don't recall what I said, but it took in the well known Gospel of John 3:16. For good measure, I followed with a short story that had come my way:

'It concerned a wealthy art collector who had one treasured son. Sorrow came with the news that he had been killed in the First World War. The art collector and his wife mourned for the rest of their days. One day a man turned up at their door, confirmed their identity, and then spoke as follows: "Your son and I were close friends. One day, I was seriously wounded in 'no-man's land'…your son saved my life and was mortally wounded in doing it. I'm not much of an artist, but at the time I made this pencil sketch of him and I wondered if you would like to have it?"

The art collector gladly accepted and in the course of time went the way of all flesh, but left instructions that his art collection was to be auctioned. An eager crowd assembled on the day, as there were some valuable items to be sold. The first picture offered was the pencil sketch…and there were no offers, but plenty of protests from the buyers. "We didn't come for that rubbish, let's have the pictures."

The auctioneer, however, persisted and eventually, to get on with the sale, someone bought it for £10 – sighs of relief, till the auctioneer announced, "I'm sorry, Ladies and Gentlemen, that is the end of the sale. My instructions are that he who gets the son, gets all." A parallel, of course, to receiving Jesus Christ the Son of God and thereby, forgiveness of sin and all that goes with it. No doubt at the auction, consternation ensued.'

The main speaker for the evening was Wyat Whyte, a mature American Southern Baptist and he also preached on *John 3:16*. I thought no more of it until, as I was leaving the building, he came to me, threw his arms about me and with emotion said, "Brother, you blessed *ma* heart tonight, that text was on *ma* heart since before *ah* left the States."

Monday morning, Billy and I, after a late night, were on our way again by six-thirty. There was little delay at the border into Hungary, but the Austrians made up for it with a 3 km queue, which pushing our luck, we jumped – only to find the Customs shut down for a full two hours, no explanation given.

It was good to get back to the excellent autobahn services facilities, personal hygiene and good eating restored. Back in Ramsgate at 4.30 a.m., we later reported to base and were diverted to pick up a car at Southampton. It was a journey in vain; the car wasn't ready, and so home without further event.

* * *

For another two or three years, I continued giving daily time at Blythswood, and enjoying a fairly active retirement. I've stopped bothering to note dates and things, but at some point, the medics decided I needed a heart pacemaker, perhaps to liven me up. I mention it simply for what I thought amusing at its installation in Raigmore hospital.

Popeşte Church – Friday afternoon, 1998

Popeşte Church – Sunday morning, 1998

Above:
Vasili on a visit to Inverness interpreting for Pastor Koval – and for Hector in Ukraine
Right:
Former hand-to-hand combat Instructor Volodia – now a Christian

Pasha, Oksana and family

Pastor Koval's wife, Vera, with her six daughters

Home Sweet Home

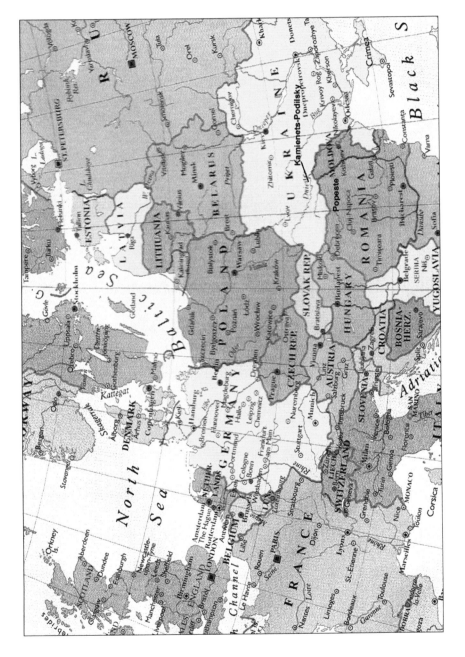

Chapter 15

Pacemaker and other things

*M*y pacemaker consists of a small electronic unit inserted just below my left shoulder. It has two leads penetrating a blood vessel and going into the heart. The operation was carried out under local anaesthetic. When the incision had been made I heard the surgeon ask for a lead, there followed a conversation something like this:

"Where did you get this from, Highland Barbed Wire Supplies?"
The reply came "It's a new kind, the first we've had."
The conversation continued.
"Lead." (The second one).
"Unit...(pause)...that looks like something from an Italian football club."
Pause
"There are no markings on the terminals."
There followed some deliberation with his assistant.
Then she said, "There's a letter beside that one."
Surgeon: "Ah, right, that'll be positive."
The unit was installed and connections made.
Surgeon: "Stitch."
I heard a mechanical click.
Surgeon: "Stitch."
Silence.
Surgeon: "Have you no more?"
Pause.
"Don't you think you should go and get some"?
I heard the sound of feet departing and returning and the job was completed. I must say that throughout I felt completely calm, confident and eventually amused.

* * *

Since I'm being light-hearted I must put on record a story that came my way recently. It concerns a Highland Region road surfacing crew who had necessity to have a temporary traffic control consisting of a couple of lollipop men with stop/go signs. It appears to have been badly timed and the morning traffic into town was being impeded. An angry motorist, a local sheriff, went from his car to a lollipop man and said, "You know what you're doing is illegal? Let me past now or there'll be more about it," or words to that effect.

There was no response and, his anger mounting, he said loudly, "Do you know who I am?"

The lollipop man turned to address his foreman, "Davy, there's a man here who doesn't know who he is."

Subsequent words and conclusion have been lost.

Tail End

Chapter 16

Introspect

*N*ow for some serious stuff, what are the regrets of my life? Some are between me and God but my greatest is certainly that I did not pay more attention to the Bible and the God of the Bible at a much earlier stage in my life. How different my life could have been.

I regret not having known my parents to any extent beyond my infancy. I regret that in earlier years I did not show the appreciation that was their due to those who made personal sacrifices to bring me up to adulthood. Besides these, there are regrets in my life for many times when my behaviour has left a lot to be desired. My present great regret is for the Godlessness that has gradually taken over our country.

Yet, I give thanks, that in spite of these, God has been unfailingly kind to me. On more occasions than I probably know, He has spared me from sudden and violent death when I wasn't ready for it. From the day of my birth on the other side of the world, throughout 78 years, He has provided for me my every need. I have never known a day without food, water, shelter and clothing. I have never been required to take a human life, a privilege not enjoyed by all my contemporaries; that is a tremendous thing. From the day I first started paid work, I have never been a day out of work till my retirement.

In spite of my frequent reluctance to conform to God's requirements from me, He has times without number impressed upon me the truth of His eternal existence, the fact of His creation of the universe in which I live and eventually my vital need of repentance and acceptance of the Lord Jesus Christ as my personal Saviour and Lord.

God blessed me with a lovely wife, Rebecca, who became a believer in our Lord Jesus Christ. We had three sons, two of whom are still here on earth and have believed from an early age. Neither of them has ever brought me a moment's trouble or anxiety.

The elder one Seoras, in terms of speed only, was a bit of a 'tearaway' on his motorbike while in his teens, but plain on his petrol tank was a bright sticker with the words from *Philippians chapter 4, verse 4*: 'Rejoice in the Lord Always'. A true believer in Christ, I knew that should his life on earth end, he would be heading straight for Heaven. His brother, Kenny, who also became a keen motorcyclist, was gifted with the most wonderful placid and caring nature. He also, in his teens became a soundly believing Christian, and they both married Christian girls.

In the period around Rebecca's sudden death, my household went from five persons to one person. It was a lonely time. I shudder to think what it would have been like without my Christian faith and the support of kind Christian people. In time and in God's providence, I became acquainted with a lovely Christian widow, Julia Goffin. Acquaintance became love, romance and marriage. I consider it God's marvellous providence that our marriage has been entirely successful and that offspring on both sides have graciously accepted the new situation.

There is not a lot more to say, except that having the experience of a life time, to anyone who has read thus far, outstandingly the most important and necessary thing you have to do, if you have not already done it, is put your life right with God.

Take a Bible and read it. It is the instruction book for life. You have been privileged with the gift of life. More than any other entity, if you ignore the instructions, the bottom line for you will be irreversibly disastrous, and that beyond measure. It is not a thing to be put off for another day. However rosy things may look, there is no guarantee of another day.

Put aside any reservations you may have, ask God to make plain to you the truth. Read, preferably first the New Testament and: 'The truth shall make you free'.

Seoras and Elizabeth

Kenny and Allison